AF485487

The Educators' Briefcase

CASES, TIPS AND TECHNIQUES FOR NAVIGATING THE EDUCATION SYSTEM

Practical Examples From the Depths of the Nation's Schools

Dorraine Reid

© 2018 Dorraine Reid
First Edition
2023 Reprint
10 9 8 7 6 5 4 3 2

All rights reserved. No part of this book may be reproduced, stored in a retrieval system, or transmitted, in any form or by any means, electronic, mechanical, photocopying, recording, or otherwise, without the prior written permission of the publishers or author.

All LMH titles, imprints and distributed lines are available at special quantity discounts for bulk purchases for sales promotions, premiums, fund-raising, educational or institutional use.

Executive Editor: K. Sean Harris
Editors: Wendy Johnson and Alcia Morgan Bromfield
Cover image: https://creativecommons.org/licenses/by/2.0/
Cover design: Sanya Dockery
Book desgin & formatting: Sanya Dockery

Published by: LMH Publishing Limited
Suite 10-11, Sagicor Industrial Park,
7 Norman Road,
Kingston C.S.O., Jamaica
Tel: 876-938-0005
Fax: 876-759-8752
Email: lmhbookpublishing@cwjamaica.com
Website: www.lmhpublishing.com

Printed in the U.S.A.   ISBN: 978-976-8245-53-3

NATIONAL LIBRARY OF JAMAICA CATALOGUING-IN-PUBLICATION DATA

Reid, Dorraine
    The educators' briefcase : cases, tips and techniques for navigating
the education system : practical examples from the depths of the
nation's schools / Dorraine Reid.

    p. ; cm
ISBN 978-976-8245-53-3 (pbk)

1. Teacher effectiveness – Jamaica   2. Teaching – Jamaica
3. Educators – Jamaica
I. Title

371.10097292   - dc 23

DEDICATION

At the heart of a challenge, lies an art to the challenge. It takes one with a heart of resilience to master the art of the challenge.

Hearts get broken; spirits get weary; challenges remain challenging.

Yet

The process of rising to a challenge remains an art to many hearts.

Dorraine Reid

To all persons taking on the educational transformation challenge and in whose lives this work will make a difference.

Acknowledgement

The author wishes to acknowledge the contribution of the following persons who assisted in the successful completion of this book:

Advisors: author and corporate trainer Margaret Spence; education administrator Liston Aiken; educator Delroy James; education administrator, Dr. Iva Bailey. Deep gratitude goes out to my editors: instructional designer Wendy Johnson; education administrator and writer, Alcia Morgan Bromfield; and proof reader, attorney-at-law and regulator, Ansord Hewitt. Special thanks is extended to Sabrena McDonald Radcliffe who assisted with the naming of this text, to all the educators who gave their testimonies to have them shared with the world through this work, and finally, to all the administrators of the various educational institutions who graciously and patiently accommodated me during my research to acquire the cases.

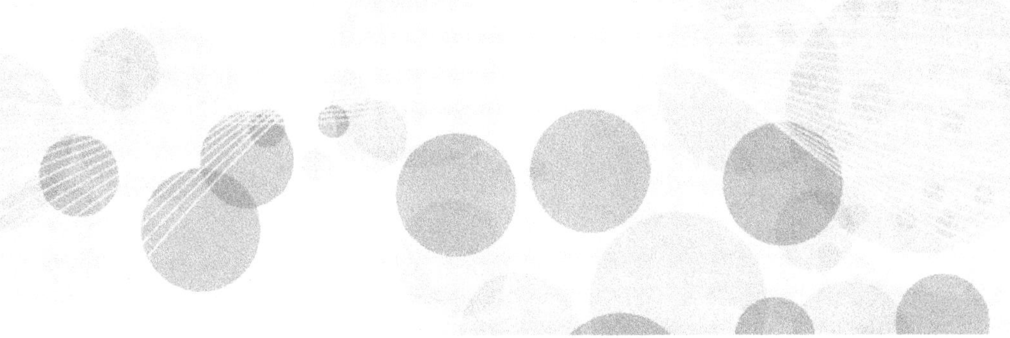

Contents

The Beginning...How Did I Get Here? xi

The Approach to Using This Book xiii

Find it in a Brief Case Study 1

PART 1: Behaviour Management 5

The Art of Behaviour Management 7

She Walked in Freely Pt. 1 9

The Supervisor 10

The Vendor 13

Graffiti on Hands 14

Doorway Bottleneck 16

Verbal Assault 18

I Am the Bigger Boss 20

He Joined Halfway 23

Classroom Management 27

The Kingdom Called 'Classroom' 29

Stolen Test Paper 33

No Specialized Training 34

The Bigger Picture 36

Frustrated Ms. Jones 38

Double Trouble with Bubble Gum 40
Out of Many One People 41
Understanding Individuality 43
Let Them Run Loose........................46
The Plot 47
Lack of Interest in Learning? 50
Mr. Technological Gadget........................51
The Confrontation 53

Administrative Management 55

Administrative Management Has its Principles 57

Jane Returns Early Pt. 2 60
...And They Got Physical 61
Throw Them Away 63
Study Leave 'Denied' 65
The Missing Cell Phone 67
Mutual Benefits........................69
Escaping the Past 71
The 'Grass' Cookies 72
Triple Threat 73
When You Go to Rome, Do as the Romans Do 76
In This Department 79
Clash of Heads........................81
How Many Chances Are Too Many?........................83
They Protested and Were Punished 86
Vending at the School Gate 88
A Clash of Wills 89
The Dismissal 92
She Knocked the Wind out of their Sails 93

PART 2: Testimonials 97

The Toolkit of Testimonial Compartment 99

From the Horse's Mouth 99
It All Happened in Ten Minutes........................100
Classroom Crack-up 103
When Being at Odds Stacked the Odds Against Them 105
Time Out in Three Minutes 107
Right Under Our Noses 110
The Day I became a Part of Their World 112
I Tried But Didn't Read Between the Lines 114

The Dismantling of Double Timetables 117

Counting Down and Raising Hands in the Name of Discipline 119

Behaviour Probation..121

PART 3: Classroom Management Tips 123

Recipes from My Classroom Menu 125

Sharing Experience 126

Musical Intro 128

Sit in Their Midst 129

Teacher's Pet 131

Movie Time 133

Grouping Methodologies 135

Additional Tips 138

PART 4 : Workshop Simulation Activities Compartment...141

Follow the Leader 144

Leader May I – Double Take 146

Let Us Do Craft..148

Do As I Say 150

Let Them Highlight It and Solve It 151

Transition Leader 152

You Made It! 155

References 157

Appendices 159

Meet the Author 170

The Beginning...

How Did I Get Here?

The idea for this book was conceived while I was addressing the final year cohort.

There I was in my element, making suggestions, providing feedback, giving advice, gaining new knowledge and answering questions, spitting eloquence. I was poised, purposeful and passionate; determined to leave a good impression and provide these 'soon to be graduates' with profound directives. Boy, was I on a roll. I felt like an expert; then I realized *I am an expert.* You have to understand the pride. I was proud that as a past student of the college, I had performed well in the field over the ten-year period, enough so that I was chosen to provide guidance to those who were where I once was.

As I stood there basking in the revelation, an unassuming young man of Grenadian nationality threw a question at me: **"How do we make these professional courses more meaningful? Whenever I go into these classes and learn about the behavioural theorists, their different strategies and all these other people, when I go into the classroom, the situation is different and some examples are not relevant. Teaching becomes frustrating."** I understood his frustration as most, if not all the texts used in the college's curriculum, were written by British or American writers and so the examples mirror those societies which in most cases are far removed from a Jamaican/Caribbean classroom. This question was greeted with consenting murmurs by some of the other students. As I listened to the discussion, the Director of Studies for the School of Drama said to me, **"Dorraine, you have heard the complaints. You were a student here and would have done some of those same courses. Having gone through the system and you are now practicing in the field, what suggestions do you have that could address this problem the students are having?"** The answer popped in my head immediately and I responded, **"I would suggest a case study approach to teaching. Actual cases that happened in the classroom so you can capture the classroom and take it to the students."** The moment the words were out of my mouth, I realized I had found a niche where I could create further impact on the education sector. As I pondered the idea, it hit me that this was not just a niche but a need that I think I could fill.   It took me some time to start the project as doubts of all nature swirled in my mind. Consequently, I was slow in getting out of the blocks, but the thought of the text would not leave my mind. Eventually, I heeded and started the process…and well, you are now holding the finished product in your hand!

The Approach to Using This Book

Professional development sessions just got more exciting...

Have you ever sat in a lecture in a stuffy, under-ventilated, over-crowded room and your body is there but your mind takes you to your favourite movie or on a hot, sunny beach with that frothy daiquiri beside you? Or worse, you are in one of those staff development seminars where the presenter drones on and you are asking yourself "Why am I here?" Too often persons complain about the monotony that comes with some of these courses or seminars that they must do. They are not averse to attending these courses but the method of delivery of content is outrageously boring.

Well, things do not have to be that way. Using the Drama strategy of role-play, facilitators of these courses can have participants role-play how they would respond to the issues in the cases contained within this text. The events that unfold during the role play could become a stimulus for a most robust discussion. This approach would fall into the Constructivist Approach which declares that "students must be actively engaged in their own learning"; this same philosophy must be applicable to training seminars. With this approach, students will get a chance to explore, justify, analyse and utilize higher order thinking skills. In addition to role play, there are lots of creative methods one can use with these cases to ensure learner participation. These include:

- Forming groups based on Gardner's Multiple Intelligences
- Blogging
- Portfolio
- Self evaluation
- Journal writing
- Videos

Facilitators should evaluate each group and apply a method that is sure to bring out the best results from it. The archaic lectures and being the "sage on the stage" will not work!

Find it in a Brief
Case Study

One of the first tools practicing teachers need is preparation. There is nothing more rewarding and inspiring than being prepared. Oh yes! With preparation, there is little room for disaster. Some teachers in training (especially the first timers) lack preparation and oftentimes walk into my classroom on their practicum with a stiff, erect posture. At times, a knife could be used to cut the tension in their bodies and voices despite their best efforts to be relaxed. On the other hand, some are a bit more relaxed and are very enthusiastic but by their third day or after the first week when they are confronted with the challenges of either managing the classroom independent of a mentor or interacting with colleagues and administrators, they quail and if administrators are not careful, they wilt under pressure, leaving students short-changed. A newly licensed teacher on his/her first job sometimes exhibit similar behaviour to a teacher in training. However, whereas teachers tend to be a little more sympathetic and helpful to teachers in training, they oftentime leave the newly employed teacher to navigate the system on his or her own. This attitude by "seasoned" teachers may be due to a number of reasons: (1) the practice teachers are under their direct supervision; (2) the licensed teacher will be held accountable for the actions of the practice teacher, and (3) a 'pass' or 'fail' concept is tied to the practicum process so help is given in an effort to help him/her to pass. However, once teachers are employed into the system, they are arguably on their own. Some schools have either an established or an informal mentoring system where new and experienced teachers are paired with each other. In other institutions, this process is totally non-existent and for many new teachers, their first year of formal teaching is like being thrown into the deep end where they may either swim or sink. The classroom is no teaching practice and teachers will encounter situations that they did not experience during their practicum. This work comes in handy and you need to keep it with you. So what exactly am I getting at?

Well...beyond this page are 'classrooms'. That's right. No jokes. Imagine that! You can enter a classroom with just the flip of a page. I am bringing the classroom to you. How you may ask? Through cases. Cases of real and potential happenings that take place in the Jamaican classroom. The cases are brief but detailed; and they are not too brief that they lack salient information. Neither are they too long so you forget the essence of them and get tired from reading them. Rather, they are comprehensive enough to hold in your 'briefcase' if you are on the go and compact with information. They are divided into three main categories: Behaviour Management, Classroom Management and Administrative Management.

Other sections of this text include testimonials which document teachers' proven and tried methods. The text also has a "Classroom Menu Kit" documented from experience. These cases do not provide the answers to everything but some of the things you need to become a more effective educator, you can find it in these brief case studies.

As noted earlier, the cases presented here are actual cases; some contain minor adjustments. The issues explored span several themes and include teacher versus teacher conflict, staff and administration, violence, defiance, differential classroom. The cases are drawn from a wide cross-section of educational institutions ranging from the affluent and well-resourced, to what is described as 'the garrison' and under resourced. Some more popular (acceptable) terms used to label some of these schools are traditional and non-traditional high schools.

The idea to package this text in "cases" was conceptualized because according to Gorton (2007), case studies are useful tools for training and professional development. A trending approach to job interviews is the use of scenarios or cases to determine the applicant's suitability for posts. More employers are using this method as an accompaniment to the somewhat clichéd questions saturating cyberspace where the answers can be easily found with the tap of a button. Therefore, if firms have adopted the practice of using role-plays during interviews to get the best, then this best practice approach of case studies must be taken to help create the best teachers.

Here's how...

- Be familiar with the various challenges educators encounter daily in the classroom.
- Be able to identify and understand issues that affect both teachers and students.
- Evaluate the seriousness of problems within the framework of the Education Code of Regulations and the Child Care and Protection Act of 2007.

Know how to...

- Respond legally, socially, morally and professionally to situations.
- Explore various approaches to handle specific problems.
- Explore best practices approach.

A suggested approach to analysing these cases include:

- Identifying the issue/s in the cases.
- Determining the cause/source of the issues.
- Identifying immediate course of action required.
- Identifying relevant persons for inclusion.
- Determining the bigger picture.
- Examining various approaches to solving the issues.
- Deciding on the most effective or appropriate of those identified.
- Explaining how the strategy is to be implemented (This is only applicable if the nature of the case calls for implementation).

Several of the issues in the cases overlap. When reading a case that is within the category of Administrative Management, you may realize that it may also have both Behaviour Management and/or Classroom Management issues. This is an indication that the education system has a composite of various parts, intricately fused together to create the perfect whole. The success of the system depends on the interaction of all its parts. It is the responsibility of educators to know how the areas are connected, and interact with them accordingly.

PART 1:

Behaviour Management

The Art of Behaviour Management

The skill of managing students' behaviour is an art every teacher must learn and keep learning because the behaviour of each student is as different as his/her fingerprints. I refer to Behaviour Management (BM) because like me, many persons think Behaviour Management is more of an art than a science because humans are not predictable like machines or the lower class of animals. Thus, teachers have to learn the dynamics of each group presented before him or her, the nuances of sub-groups within that group, and the peculiarities of the individuals within the group. In doing so, such a teacher will be more equipped to deal effectively with the idiosyncrasies that his/her students show up with daily.

There are established ideas about how a teacher may go about managing students' behaviour; many of which are rooted in the theories of behaviourists, psycho-therapists, psychologists and sociologists. Oftentimes, these theories take precedence over the actual experience of the classroom practitioners themselves. This often leads to deep controversy as these theories are not necessarily the most suitable point of reference at that time. Sometimes even practitioners do not give much credence to their own tried and proven work.

Pragmatic Behaviour Management, dictates that the purpose of the behaviour being sought has students at the centre of this purpose. However, in some Jamaican schools, students are often warned to behave and not bring the school's name into disrepute. While protecting the school's name is important, it is the student who must ultimately derive personal benefit. One cannot have students being asked to behave well to avoid the school getting a bad name; this cannot be the primary reason for behaving in an acceptable manner. This message of behaving well for the school's sake is a way of asking students to do some 'masking' until they are free to unmask when the school's name is not at stake. Pragmatic Behaviour Management therefore postures the view that when one is advocating for genuine behaviour change, the preservation of the school's name should not be a primary reason.

Probably Behaviour Management needs to be seen as part of a behaviour transformation or a maturation continuum. Along this continuum, students should be made aware of where their behaviour is, where it needs to be, and how they need to get there. The teacher is accepted as enabler/facilitator towards this behaviour goal. The process is then a partnership involving the student, school and parent. In this partnership, the parties agree on the ground rules as a constant point of reference. They review, dialogue and discuss so each time a class meets, conduct forms a central part of expectations.

This book has drawn from the experience of a number of educational practitioners on this matter of Behaviour Management. Their cases are tried and proven and remains the most reliable point of reference for today's practitioners.

Liston Aiken
Education Administrator

BM #1:
She Walked in Freely Pt. I

It was 12:40 p.m. It was the penultimate session of the school day at Bethal Heights High School for girls. One of the school's rules stipulated that no student should be out of class during this time unless she had a corridor pass. Mr. Brown was conducting his social studies class with students of grade 8-1. It was a double session and was slated to end at 2:00 p.m. Half an hour into the first session, as he sat at his desk at the front of the class waiting on the young ladies to complete a given task, two students appeared at the door. One of the students, Jane Doherty, entered his classroom and walked by his desk. Taken aback, he looked in the direction of the young lady and inquired about her purpose inside his classroom. She ignored him and then went to stand beside a student. Only then did she turn to Mr. Brown and ask, "Sir, may I talk to my cousin?"

"No you may not. How dare you walk into my class without first seeking permission to do so?" Mr. Brown responded sternly. Jane, seemingly dissatisfied with the response, proceeded to stare disapprovingly at Mr. Brown. He stared at Jane, then looked at the students who had by this time stopped working and were paying keen attention to Mr. Brown and Jane. "You are disrupting my class, young lady. Please leave," he instructed and stood up. Jane stood there defiantly for a moment and then marched away angrily past Mr. Brown who was at his desk. He then instructed her to go to the office and wait until he arrived.

QUESTIONS FOR DISCUSSION:

1. What are the issues in this case?
2. Were you Mr. Brown, how would you proceed with your class following the disruption?

3. What actions would you have taken to ensure Jane left your class?

4. Are Jane's actions a breach of any school rules?

5. Was Mr. Brown wrong in denying Jane's request to speak to her cousin?

6. Is there anything in the Education Code of Regulations or the Child Protection Act that addresses the issues present in the case?

BM #2:
The Supervisor

Marcia Smith has been working at Happy Gail High School for twelve years. She has always displayed good work ethics. She is always punctual for work, maintains accurate administrative records for her students, and is a stern disciplinarian who encourages her students and implements appropriate measures to ensure they adhere to school rules. She also maintains a healthy rapport with her colleagues and helps them to achieve their goals; actively participates in extra-curricular activities; willingly takes on leadership roles for non-academic activities; and sees to the welfare of the students. All these characteristics have elevated her to the position of senior teacher with special responsibility as a grade supervisor for grade 11, a post she has held for the past two years. One morning as she was supervising the staff and students during assembly, the following occurred:

(Student Kacey Mills steps out of line and begins to talk to her friend.)

Ms. Smith: Young lady, please step back in the line.

Kacey: I am comfortable right here.

Ms. Smith: Excuse me? This is not about where you are comfortable. All students are supposed to form a straight line and all your classmates are standing in the line except you. Please go and stand in the line.

(*Kacey did not answer, neither did she move to the line.*)

Young lady, I am speaking to you.

Kacey: Miss, I said I am comfortable right here. I am not moving.

(*Ms. Smith informs the form teacher for Kacey's class that she should not go to the classroom with the other students. She then realizes that Kacey is wearing a green elastic band in her hair.*)

Ms. Smith: You are also wearing the wrong colour band in your hair. Please remove it.

Kacey: Miss, I don't have anything else to use.

Ms. Smith: You know the rules. Is green one of the colours allowed with your uniform? (*Kacey does not respond.*) Young lady, remove the green elastic band from your hair.

Kacey: Are you going to give me something to catch up my hair when I remove it? (*She stares defiantly at Ms. Smith.*)

The rest of Kacey's classmates were allowed to proceed to their classroom without her. Just then Mr. Denton Everest, who is also a grade eleven supervisor arrived, saw the student standing outside and inquired of Ms. Smith what had happened. Mr. Everest has been the grade eleven supervisor for the past six years and has been working at Happy Gail High for twenty-two years. Ms. Smith explained to Mr. Everest that the student Kacey Mills has been outrightly disrespectful to her and showed scant regards for the school rules. He left to speak with the student. While speaking to her, Kacey removed the green elastic band from her hair, retrieved from her pocket the appropriate colour and placed it in her hair.

The following day, Kacey returned to school with the green elastic band in her hair. She attempted to join the line with her classmates but Ms. Smith saw the green elastic band and Kacey was asked to step out of the line. This time the matter was addressed by Mr. Everest.

Mr. Everest: Why did you wear that green thing back to school?

> (*No answer*)

Mr. Everest: I'm talking to you young lady.

> (*Still silent*)

Mr. Everest: You wore it yesterday and you were spoken to. I know you have the appropriate colour so I would like you to explain why you have decided to be defiant.

Kacey: That woman must stop see me. Weh she a pick pon me fah? She need fi stop see me. (*Hisses her teeth*)

Mr. Everest: Who are you calling 'that woman'? And who are you hissing your teeth at? (*Silence*) You are very rude. You were logged yesterday for this behaviour and you have returned today with the same thing. I will have to send for your parents and you will also be suspended. Your action is clearly a deliberate attempt to defy authority. At this institution we maintain law and order. If you have a problem with the rules, then your parents will have to find somewhere else for you because we will not change the rules to suit you.

QUESTIONS FOR DISCUSSION:

1. Do you think Kacey should have been punished from the first day she wore the incorrect colour band in her hair?

2. If you were Ms. Smith, what would be your reaction to the situation on day 1?

3. Do you think Kacey's parents should have been notified from the first incident?

4. How would you describe Mr. Everest's handling of the situation in both cases?

5. Is there anything in the Education Code of Regulation or Child Protection Act that speaks to the issues in this case?

BM #3:

The Vendor

Blenda Mullings is an 'A' student and has been that way since first form. However, she is from the lower socioeconomic stratum of society so she has difficulty with her finances. Since third form, she has resorted to selling things, thus she is known by the grade ten (10) cohort as "The Venda". On a daily basis, transactions would take place discreetly as vending is against the school's rules.

It was social studies period and Ms. Grenshaw was late for class as usual. Upon her arrival, she saw a crowd gathered in one corner of the room – some had monies in their hands; one girl was shouting: "I want a red one", another "I want a 32B", and yet another, "How much me owe you?"

Shocked, she approached the group and saw Blenda in the midst with a bag filled with brassieres. Aghast, Ms. Grenshaw confiscated the bag and later took it to the principal's office. Blenda was only given a strong warning but the items were not returned to her.

Two weeks later, Blenda's mom came to see Ms. Grenshaw about the confiscation of the items. A heated argument developed where Blenda's mom tried to explain that the sale from the items helped to send her daughter to school as she was a single, unemployed mother. Ms. Grenshaw told her the rules were the rules regardless. This riled Blenda's mother even more and she began to hurl expletives at the teacher. Just then the principal came on the scene and asked both parties to meet her in her office.

QUESTIONS FOR DISCUSSION:

1. Discuss the possible reasons why the student had the chance to sell during class time.

2. Was the teacher justified in confiscating the items?

3. Do you believe the items should have been returned to the student? If so, when would be the appropriate time?

4. Why do you believe an argument developed between Ms. Grenshaw and the student's parent?

5. Is the parent's arguments justified?

6. Based on the issues identified, do you see the need for any professional development sessions? State what these are.

7. Do you see the need for any professional development initiative/workshop? If so, what would it be about?

8. Is there anything in the Education Code of Regulations or Child Care and Protection Act that speaks to the issues in the case?

BM #4:
Graffiti on Hands

Marsha Wright sat quietly in Mrs. Black's math class with a blank stare. She refused to participate in the activities despite Mrs. Black's encouragement. The teacher thought it better to leave Marsha alone and continue with her class as end of year examinations were just two weeks away and she was behind in completing the syllabus. While Mrs. Black continued, Marsha took a black marker from her bag and on her arm in all caps she wrote "F@#$%%$ all of you". Jane who sat next to Marsha alerted Mrs. Black to this action who then asked Marsha to come to her desk.

(Marsha does not move.)

Mrs. Black*:* Marsha, I am waiting on you.

(Marsha hisses her teeth.)

Mrs. Black: As a matter of fact, let us both step outside briefly.
(She walks to the door.)

Marsha: Miss, me a tell yuh de truth, if I step outside I'm not stepping back inside.

Mrs. Black: It is okay Marsha, we can also discuss that when we step outside.

Marsha: Miss you hear what me say though? Me nah move till you say you undastan cause when me nuh come back, a you first a go talk say me step outta you class and gone.

Jane: *(Under her breath)* Watch yah, she brite eeh? A mussi she a principal.

Marsha: Hey gal how you can chat so? Nobody a talk to you? You fi learn fi mine you own business.
(Jane hisses her teeth.)

Marsha: Hey gyal…
(She throws a book and hits Jane on the shoulder. Mrs. Black goes to restrain her.)

Mrs. Black then took a seething Marsha outside and demanded to know what was going on. She questioned Marsha about the writing on her hand to which Marsha replied defiantly, "Is my hand and I write what I want to write on it."

"Marsha I asked you a question," Mrs. Black repeated.

"Better you don't ask me nutten Miss," was her swift response.

With that, Mrs. Black escorted Marsha to the principal's office and Jane was sent to the nurse's station for examination.

The principal called Marsha's mother who indicated that she was unable to make it to school at the moment or that day for that matter. She further expressed that she has had enough of Marsha's behaviour. After the conversation with the student's mother, the principal sat quietly for a few minutes contemplating what to do. Eventually, she sent Marsha to the guidance counsellor's office.

QUESTIONS FOR DISCUSSION:

1. Can you identify the issues in this case?
2. Do you agree with Jane for reporting Marsha's actions to the teacher?
3. What could Mrs. Black have done differently at the beginning of the class?
4. Provide strategies that Mrs. Black could employ to get a different outcome.
5. What can you infer about Marsha's situation based on her parent's response?
6. Is there an underlying meaning to Marsha's behaviour?
7. Is there anything in the Education Code of Regulations or Child Care and Protection Act that speaks to the issues in the case?

BM#5:
Doorway Bottleneck

Ms. Willis, form teacher for 7-3 was late for work again and so her class was being manned by Year Supervisor Mrs. Gerald during the devotion period. Three students, Mary-Lee, Shania and Lisa, chatted incessantly despite instructions from Mrs. Gerald to listen to what was being said over the intercom. After three attempts to get them to conform, she eventually put them to stand outside the classroom door. Mary-Lee's blouse was out of her skirt and so she was sent to the bathroom to adjust her attire. A displeased Mary-Lee hissed her teeth and flounced away. When the bell rang to signal the close of the devotional exercise, both Shania and Lisa were allowed to go back to their seats. Mrs. Gerald stood at the doorway and was addressing the class about their conduct when Mary-Lee returned. Without saying "Excuse me" she shoved her way past Mrs. Gerald. The contact caused Mrs. Gerald to stagger. Mrs. Gerald steadied herself and grabbed Mary-Lee by her collar from behind and pulled her back through the door. She then instructed Mary-Lee to enter the room the appropriate way. Mary-Lee once more shoved past Mrs. Gerald less aggressively, but bounced her again. Once more Mrs. Gerald pulled her back and repeated the instructions. This time Mary-Lee mumbled, "Excuse me". Mrs. Gerald stepped away from the door and Mary-Lee entered. The students giggled. An angry and embarassed Mary-Lee complained about being bullied by Mrs. Gerald and indicated she would be taking her parents to school the following day.

The following morning, the vice principal called Mrs. Gerald to her office. Both Mary-Lee and her parents were there. The vice principal asked for an explanation. Following the verbal explanation, she asked Mrs. Gerald for the record of the incident in her log book. Mrs. Gerald had not made a notation of the incident. She then went to the class to get the students' view on what had happened and while there, she addressed all the students of Ms. Willis' class about their need to be respectful and display social graces.

QUESTIONS FOR DISCUSSION:

1. Did Mrs. Gerald handle the situation appropriately?

2. Discuss the action of the student Mary-Lee.

3. What would you have done differently if you had been Mrs. Gerald?

4. What would be your next step if you were in Mrs. Gerald's position?

5. What do you believe the vice principal should tell the parents?

6. What action, if any, should be taken against the teacher who was late?

7. Do you see the need for any professional development initiative/workshop? If so, what would it be about?

8. Is there anything in the Education Code of Regulations or Child Care and Protection Act that speaks to the issue(s) identified in the case?

BM # 6:
Verbal Assault

Ms. Stewart was in her social studies class the first period Monday morning. The classroom had limited seating so some students were standing. The lesson had begun on time. Thirty minutes into the lesson, Brittany Coupeland asked if she could go and use the bathroom. Ms. Stewart granted her the permission to do so. Mitsy Richards, who was one of the students standing, moved to sit in the chair Brittany vacated.

Upon Brittany's return, Mitsy got up immediately and went back to stand in the corner against the bookshelf. Seeing Mitsy getting up from the chair, a seething Brittany grabbed a book and started fanning the chair aggressively while simultaneously blowing exaggerated puffs of air with her mouth on it.

"Just what do you think you are doing"? inquired Ms. Stewart.

"Cleaning the chair because I don't want to catch any germs" was Brittany's quick response. Mitsy heard and countered with:

"Watch yah! Hey gal, you have more germs than me. You think you better than me?" She hissed her teeth loudly. "You black and ugly and dunce like. Me way brighter and cleaner than you."

"You chat too much. Who ask you nutten? Nobody nah chat to you ole germsy, germsy skin gal. You too damn nuff. I hate har you see man." She hissed her teeth and both continued to yell.

Ms. Stewart instructed both girls to stop the quarrelling, yet they continued to curse on top of their voices. Ms. Stewart then asked them both to step outside the classroom and stay by the door until the end of the class.

The school's dean of discipline was passing by and saw Brittany sitting on the staircase and inquired of her the reason for not being in class. Brittany explained that she had been sent out of the class by Ms. Stewart. A puzzled dean decided to inquire of Ms. Stewart what had happened as it was against the school rule and education policy to send a child away from the classroom to be on his or her own. When she got to the classroom and saw Mitsy standing just outside the door, she instructed her to go inside the class. Mitsy explained that she was on punishment and that was why she was there.

The dean then went inside the room and sat for the rest of the session. At the end of the session, she inquired why the girls had been sent outside. Upon hearing Ms. Stewart's account, she expressed deep concern that Brittany had been out of her (Ms. Stewart's) eye sight. Ms. Stewart pointed out that both girls were told specifically to stand at the classroom door. The dean then asked Brittany why had she gone to sit on the steps instead of stand at the classroom door as she had been instructed. Her response was that she didn't wish to stand next to Mitsy. Besides her feet were tired so she decided to go and sit. Brittany was asked about her reason for lying about being sent outside by Ms. Stewart. She hung her head and explained softly that she did not want to get into trouble.

QUESTIONS FOR DISCUSSION:

1. What previous event(s) could possibly have led to the girls behaving the way they did in the classroom?

2. Establishing 'ground rules or class rules' at the beginning of the school year is of paramount importance to class control. Do you think this was done by the teacher? Why/Why not?

3. Do you think the course of action taken by Ms. Stewart is appropriate?

4. Is there anything you think Ms. Stewart could have done differently to prevent the situation from escalating?

5. Did the dean act appropriately when she went to sit inside Ms. Stewart's class?

6. What action, if any, do you think should be taken against the girls?

7. As the school's education officer, what advice would you give to Ms. Stewart?

8. Is there anything in the Education Code of Regulations and/or Child Care and Protection Act that speaks to the issue(s) in this case?

BM #7:
I Am The Bigger Boss

Gordon Road Primary and Junior High School is a co-educational institution located in an inner city area and is surrounded by what is called garrison communities where persons have strong loyalty to one political party. The rules are somewhat different from the rules of the land and the community members answer to a 'don' who acts as the 'godfather' of the area. Most of the students who attend the school are from the surrounding communities and often display the characteristics of garrison life hence, the staff, administration and school board try to provide strong, positive leadership to the students and form bonds with the residents of the surrounding communities. Despite this, the school has been plagued with sporadic outbursts of gang related incidents among the students.

Martina, a grade nine student, is the leader of a gang called 'BOSS', an acronym for 'Bad, Official, Sassy and Sexy'. The group comprises five girls of varying ages from fourteen to seventeen. Martina is the oldest at seventeen and has spent two years already in grade nine. This is her last year. Since grade eight she has been suspended on numerous occasions for disruptive behaviour that often resulted in physical altercations. She has also displayed violent behaviour that required the intervention of the police. She is a fixture at the Guidance and Counselling Centre and has her own officer from the Child Development Agency (CDA). Her sister, Michelle, is in grade eight. Whenever Michelle has an argument with her peers, she would often go to her sister Martina, who would go to the grade eight block and start a fight in defence of her sister.

On the last day of the Easter term, the school had its annual fair. All the students and community members turned up dressed in the latest fashion. On their return to school, the grade eight students milled around the school yard discussing among themselves the various attires they had seen at the fair. During the discussion, they expressed opinions about the individuals they thought looked fab and those who looked drab. Michelle overheard a part of a discussion and went to the grade nine block to complain to her sister Martina, that the grade eight girls made both she and her fall in the 'drab' category.

The grade eight girls had to walk by the grade nine block to go to their first class of the day. On their way to the chemistry lab, BOSS, led by Martina, insisted that the grade eight girls ask permission to pass. The girls refused and a brief fight erupted. Mr. Harvey, the chemistry teacher, came out and with the help of some of the boys, managed to pull the girls apart and stop the melee. Despite this, and totally ignoring the presence of the teacher, the girls hurled harsh threats laced with expletives at one another. The vice principal (VP) who was on her way to do an assessment of Mr. Harvey, saw what transpired and ordered the girls into the chemistry lab.

VP: What kind of undisciplined display is this on the school's grounds? Haven't you learnt anything from your previous suspensions or from the talks from the school's resource officers?

Vanessa: Miss, you see how dem a ask fi trouble? Mi a waan you enuh Miss. Mi ago do one a dem supm enuh! *(She took a compass from her bag.)*

VP: Vanessa Greaves, stop your foolishness. Give that to me and just calm down and explain what happened. *(Her face was set and the girls knew that look and knew she would not stop until she wrung the truth from them.)*

Shereen: Miss, that gal always a come pick fight wid we and we nuh trouble har. But Miss, me nah run from har. Me a go damage har. Why me must ask her permission to pass grade nine and is not her yard? Is not har pupa own de school!

VP: If you girls continue to behave this way, we will not get anywhere and you will get yourselves in double trouble. Do not throw away your right. As for you Ms. Vanessa, you just won an award with the JCDC Festival Speech and Drama Competition for the school. Do you want to lose that honour?

Vanessa: Miss me just angry! Everyday is the same thing. Is the one Michelle carry we name to them and now dem a come pick fight. But Miss, me a warn you. Talk to dem because me a go hurt one of them. Ohhh.

VP: (*Chuckled, shook her head and reached for the compass.*) Martina is in enough trouble with the school as it is. Don't allow her to pull you into that. She has been doing quite well especially since the new school resource officer began to work with her. Come with me ladies, let us go to the office of the dean to sort this mess out. Mr. Harvey, please continue with your class. These two will be late.

The vice principal left with the girls in tow to her office. By the time the dean arrived, they had calmed down. Both administrators listened to the girls' story then sent to call Martina and her "friends". A sheepish Martina walked in followed by a scared bunch of four. They admitted Michelle told them the girls had said some negative things about them and that was the reason Martina suggested that course of action. Some of the girls admitted they didn't want to do it but Martina said they would be kicked out of the group if they didn't participate. Martina was threatened with a suspension and was placed on probation. The dean reminded her that were she to get one more suspension, she could be expelled. Michelle was warned about inciting violence. They were sent to the principal who gave them a letter to take home which informed their parents of the incident and invited them to a meeting the following day.

The sisters lived with both parents. The principal opted to address the letter to the mother as she was quite strict and tried to get the girls to obey school rules while the father was a permissive parent who would take the girls to parties and have them stay late into the night even when it was a school night.

QUESTIONS FOR DISCUSSION:

1.   What are the main issues?

2. Did the school attempt enough intervention strategies for Martina?

3. Given Martina's behaviour history, should she still have been in that institution?

4. Did the school take any /enough measures to nullify the actions of Michelle?

5. Should the school have taken any other action against Michelle? If yes, what should that action be?

6. Do you believe the background of the children has anything to do with their behaviour?

7. Is there anything in the Education Code of Regulations and/or Child Care and Protection Act that addresses the issue(s) in the case?

BM #8
He Joined Halfway

Sixteen-year old Sean Mitchell and his mother moved to Kingston in 2008. After his father died his mother wanted to move away from the community and had sought and received a new job in Kingston. There was no one for his mother to leave Sean with in the country, hence he had to relocate to Kingston with her. She applied for a transfer to Knotewell Academy and he was accepted and placed in grade ten. Knotewell Academy is an institution geared towards building the academic and disciplinary standards of students who are struggling in the regular school system.

The principal, in her review of Sean's last report from his previous school, noted that he was performing below average and had received very low grades in five of eight subject areas. She also observed that the comments from the teachers indicated that Sean lacked focus and wasted a lot of time in and out of class. She decided to try with him however, based on the school's mission statement "To Help Where Others Have Given Up".

For the first term, Sean settled in and tried to improve his academics but was struggling as he lacked the foundation. In January, a noted change was seen in his behaviour. On February 23, 2009, Marsha Bogle, a prefect, reported to the dean of discipline that during the lunch break, she was standing under the trees with her friends, when Sean approached the group and proceeded to gyrate on her buttocks. Sean was called to the dean's office where he was strongly reprimanded for his actions. When he left the dean's office, he went in search of Marsha and hit her repeatedly in the face for making the complaint. The matter was reported to the principal and Sean was suspended for five days. He was given a letter for his mother which asked him to return with her to appear before the personnel committee of the school board.

He matriculated to grade eleven even though his grades had not improved. On October 14, 2009, he was suspended for three days for disrespectful behaviour to a teacher. His parent was asked to come in and see the principal.

January 18, 2010, Sean was once again placed on five days in-house suspension for bullying a ninth grade student and openly disobeying the directives of his year supervisor.

March 1, 2010, he was seen wearing a pair of earrings and was asked by the principal to remove it as it was not a part of his uniform and thus was not allowed. He openly indicated that he would not remove them and walked away. He was placed on five days suspension and asked to return after the five days with his parent.

Several days after he resumed school, Sean was seen using a cellular phone in the school's canteen. The vice principal beckoned to him to turn over the phone to which he responded definitively that he would not give it up and proceeded with his conversation. He was asked repeatedly to do so and he didn't. He was suspended for ten days and his case referred to the School Board. The Board decided that with all the past cases and this recent defiance, he ought to be expelled.

QUESTIONS FOR DISCUSSION:

1. Should the school have admitted him based on the details of his last school report?

2. Should there have been a probationary contract? How binding can it be viz-a-viz the UN Charter of Rights of the Child?

3. Should the school's administrators have had any intervention strategies for reformation either at the beginning of, or during Sean's two years?

4. Did the administrators follow proper procedures in their disciplinary measures?

5. Is there anything in the Education Code of Regulation and/or Child Care and Protection Act that addresses the issue(s) identified in the case?

6. Based on issues identified and actions taken, do you see the need for professional development strategies? If so, state them.

Classroom Management

The Kingdom Called Classroom

I will not expend the energies to give a definition of classroom management as several scholars have posited various definitions for this terminology and whereas all of them may not agree as to what the "correct" definition is, a fundamental thing to note is that their definitions all have similar underlying meaning or suggested purpose. For example, according to the Handbook of Classroom Management: Research, Practice and Contemporary Issues by Evertson and Weinstein (2006), classroom management has two distinct purposes: To establish and sustain an orderly environment so students can engage in meaningful academic learning, and also to aim to enhance student social and moral growth.

Fundamental to this definition is that teachers should manage their class-rooms and do so effectively. I believe all educators should re-orient their thinking and not see themselves as mere teachers but managers. Yes! That's right. Education managers. The teaching profession can then be viewed as a whole conglomerate by itself because teachers are managers of time, content, people, behaviour, process and the list goes on. When teachers begin to think of themselves as managers, they will take a holistic approach to their substantive tasks and the multiplicity of roles they play in the education process. These roles and tasks can occur within and without the walls of the classroom. The classroom is not the teacher. It is not the students and it is certainly not the building. Why not, you ask? The answer is simple really...teachers need someone to teach or facilitate; students need someone to facilitate them and lastly, teaching and learning does not always take place inside a building. Education managers then must remain cognizant of this fact and treat the education of students as a process whether or not they are within the ambit of a classroom. For effective teaching and learning, there has to be clarity and efficiency.

Please note that if a classroom is not properly managed, then effective teaching and learning will only be an elusive concept desired by many. A properly managed classroom then refers to the design and enforcement of rules, regulations and procedures to guide actions. If these are absent, negative behaviours such as chaos, disruption, disorder and even disrespect may reign supreme as 'lord' and 'king' in the kingdom called classroom. When these undesirables take charge of the teaching and learning space, the business of education will become difficult and teachers may struggle desperately to impart knowledge or change behaviour to the desired conduct. Students may not be engaged in the learning process,and hence may not grasp adequate content; the result of which can be frustration and demotivation for both parties. Conversely, a well-managed classroom results in productive teaching and learning; eager, enthusiastic students; motivated, inspired teachers, the result of which can be excellence in education. May I point out here that productivity in the classroom is not easily achieved with the wave of a magic wand or utterances over a crystal ball. Far from it! Productivity takes hard work which includes collaboration, reinforcement, and clear, achievable goals. Being an effective class/education manager therefore is not a hereditary trait that inevitably eludes some persons; more so, it is a choice that educators must make; a choice that will help them grow as they develop in this role.

Being a good classroom manager is not as difficult as it may seem and neither is it a walk in the park. However, with consistent practice, you will eventually become an expert at it. Following are some basic guidelines that a teacher needs to set him/herself on the path to becoming an effective classroom manager.

Establish expected patterns of behaviour for both your students and yourself. Do this with the input of students as this will give them the opportunity to see themselves as more than mere subjects but as subjects with voices and equal privileges in this kingdom. They will also see you as more than "General King-Kong" but more so as a human being who takes their input into consideration.

Make only those promises you can afford to deliver on and follow through on them. Whether it is a promise of reward or punishment, it sends a message to students that you mean business.

Be consistent. For e.g., if you have a rule that students should form a line before entering your classroom, stick with it and do it all the time and with everyone. This will help students learn the culture of your classroom. Sooner or later you will not have to tell them what to do and by employing consistency, your job becomes easier. Students need structure and consistency helps to create structure.

Ensure you plan interesting and exciting lessons that keep students engaged. If students are bored, they will become disruptive or sleep in your class. Your lessons should be planned in such a way that your students are actively involved in the learning process. Make sure lessons are student-centred so it is not about what you will do but more about what the students will do and how they will do it.

Lessons should not only be exciting but they must be at a level of complexity that is appropriate for the age group. In other words, they should not be too simple and they should not be too difficult. The degree of difficulty should be at a level where students are challenged in the process but the tasks are not beyond their abilities to grasp and comprehend.

Ensure particular life skills are employed by students such as the ability to manage time through tasks given, make notes without being prompted, become respectful, and attend classes on time.

Create and utilize special coding procedures. For example, when the teacher holds up his/her right hand, students know that they should all go quiet. The teacher may also employ a counting methodology where he/she counts from one to three. These must be understood by students and established at the beginning of a class if they are to be effective.

This list is by no means exhaustive but the concepts are basic strategies that the beginning or practicing education manager could start with. I am sure you will explore others that are more intermediate and advanced. In this kingdom called the classroom, management is flexible and allows each educator to stamp his or her own creativity and style on it. Just remember, the aim is to effectively manage the classroom or should I say the teaching and learning environment.

Happy teaching!

CM #1:
Stolen Test Paper

It was time for the first set of internal assessments and Mr. Brown decided to administer a biology test to his two sets of grade 10 students. At 8:30 he went to his first class, 10-5. The class lasted an hour. At 9:30 a.m., he collected the test papers separately from answer sheets and while he sat at the teacher's desk putting his things together to go to the next class, he was approached by one of his past students, Melissa, who was now in grade 11. They became engaged in dialogue when the student inconspicuously removed one of the test papers from his desk.

He later made his way to grade 10-7 for their 10:30 a.m. to 11:30 a.m. session during which time he would administer the test. He entered the room and said good morning but was unnoticed by a group of students who were huddled around a desk. Mr. Brown went to investigate. When they saw him, they became shocked and frantic, and in their confusion, they scattered and threw the paper on the ground. Taking up the paper, he realized it was the test that he was about to administer. A visibly shocked and upset Mr. Brown did an on the spot investigation and it was revealed that Melissa had given it to them. Mr. Brown took the group of girls to the office and sent for Melissa and postponed the administration of the test.

QUESTIONS FOR DISCUSSION:

7. Did Mr. Brown do the right thing by taking the girls to the office and refusing to administer the test?

8. What strategies would you employ to prevent a reoccurrence?

9. What other course of action would you take besides taking the girls to the office?

10. Some would argue that Mr. Brown was negligent in his actions in the first class. What do you think?

11. Is there anything in the Education Code of Regulations/Child Care and Protection Act that addressed the issue(s) identified in the case? If there isn't, what school rule do you think could be used to address this?

CM #2:
No Specialized Training

Mr. Pitman, the school's drama teacher, has been asked to work with a special group of 7th grade students. There are ten males and three females in the group. These students are known for a variety of emotional and behavioural challenges and have been assigned a special timetable that offers extra math, English, drama, music and information technology. At the start of the second term, when the administration designed their timetable and selected the teachers to give the extra session, they had promised that another member of staff would be assigned to help monitor the students' conduct during the session. All the teachers who were selected to work with the students were asked to make monthly reports to the grade coordinator, vice-principal and principal. The teachers had been assured that the sole guidance counsellor would put together a list of strategies to be used to help improve the students' learning as some of the teachers did not have the specialized training required to attend to the needs of the students.

Mr. Pitman has this class for drama immediately after lunch every Wednesday. The bell indicating the time for class to begin had sounded. Mr. Pitman had since made three trips to the door to remind the students to line up outside the room as this was a stipulation from the principal. Only seven of the thirteen students were present. Mr. Pitman, having felt how hot it was outside, decided to allow them to enter. He had gotten accustomed to some of the students being late. He got the students settled in their seats and suggested he would allow a three-minute grace period before he started the activity.

He proceeded to take the register. After the first name was called, two students entered. They failed to acknowledge Mr. Pitman but instead interrupted the students with tales about what had happened during lunch. It took Mr. Pitman fifteen minutes to get through marking the names of the nine students who were present. With only thirty of forty-five minutes remaining for the session, Mr. Pitman set out to get the first learning exercise going. During the instructions, the remaining four boys entered. One rushed to the window at the opposite side of the room muttering something about one student having stolen something. Another moved toward the last two who came in just prior to him. They were evidently happy to see one another, seemingly anxious to share details about some story unknown to the teacher. The third boy sat on a desk at the back completely consumed by the delight of his chips and juice. The fourth went to sit in his seat without causing further fuss. Mr. Pitman, after several minutes of trying to get the students settled and failing to get through articulating one sentence of instructions for the starter activity, walked out of the room and headed to the administrative office. The supporting staff he was promised still had not turned up nor were the suggestions from the guidance counsellor forthcoming.

QUESTIONS FOR DISCUSSION:

6. What are some classroom management strategies that Mr. Pitman could employ to help control the behaviour of the students in the class?

7. What do you think was Mr. Pitman's main concern?

8. Do you believe Mr.Pitman did enough to try to control the students' behaviour?

9. If you were the supervisor or principal handling this institution, how would you address Mr.Pitman's concerns?

10. Do you think Mr.Pitman contributed to these students being constantly late for his class? If so, how?

11. Should Mr. Pitman have been made to teach this class without the supervision of a specialist?

12. How would you describe the guidance counsellor's actions?

13. Should these students be placed in the main education system?

14. Is there anything in the Education Code of Regulations that addresses the issue(s) identified in the case?

15. Conduct a needs assessment to ascertain if there is need for any professional development training based on the issue(s) in the case.

CM #3:
The Bigger Picture

For over a month, every Thursday, period 2, Mr. Thomas, the technical drawing and music teacher, can expect Mrs. Ennis to stop by, not for a friendly chat but to ask him if he could keep Martin Blythe, a grade 8 student for the remainder of the session. He didn't mind keeping Martin and tried to keep him occupied with drawing activities, playing around with musical instruments or having little chats about current affairs, or whatever was on Martin's mind. He was now growing concerned about the frequency with which this was happening and decided to make the grade supervisor aware of the situation.

Later that day, fearing backlash, Mr. Thomas informed Mrs. Ennis that he had made the grade supervisor aware that he had been hosting Martin. He was surprised that Mrs. Ennis wasn't furious with him. Apparently, for some of the other English periods, Mrs. Ennis sends Martin to the office or to the grade coordinator. Mrs. Ennis, a petite, well-spoken and immaculately attired young lady, explained she was unaccustomed to working in an inner-city school. She had just graduated and this was the only school that had responded to her hundreds of applications.

Having accepted the job, she found that most of the students showed very little interest in her classes. She described most of the students as being loud and aggressive and thought that attempts to get them to write and speak in standard English was a waste of time. She lamented that despite her best efforts she was just not able to get Martin to sit through an entire lesson more so to attempt assigned tasks. She mentioned that whenever she tried to get his attention or offer any form of correction it seemed to make him angry. What she found most frustrating was that she was not able to connect with Martin, or seemed to be reaching him on any level. She has made countless reports about his behaviour and even tried making contact with his guardian but nothing seemed to be helping.

As Mr. Thomas watched Mrs. Ennis agonize over feelings of inadequacy, he felt an urge to ask her if she knew anything of the student's background. He was stunned that she was ignorant of the fact that Martin had lost his father a few years ago to a brutal killing and only a year ago his mother went missing and still had not been found.

QUESTIONS FOR DISCUSSION:

9. Do you believe Mrs. Ennis had made enough effort to work with Martin? What evidence is given which supports your answer?

10. Do you think she will survive in the classroom?

11. What positives, if any, does Mrs. Ennis have going for her?

12. If you were Mr. Thomas, what advice would you give to Mrs. Ennis when you realize she was ignorant of the student's background?

13. What classroom or behaviour management strategies could Mrs. Ennis attempt to use to help Martin focus in class?

14. How do you think the school can help Martin?

15. Do you believe Martin's actions could affect his classmates? If yes, how so?

16. Why was Mr. Thomas able to engage Martin?

17. What difference do you think it would have made if Mrs. Ennis had known about Martin's background?

18. Could Martin's background be a contributor to his behaviour? Explain.

19. In cases like this, should teachers be informed of a student's background? Whose responsibility should it be?

20. Conduct a needs assessment to ascertain if there is need for any professional development training based on the issue(s) in the case.

CM #4:
Frustrated Ms. Jones

Ms. Francene Jones has been a teacher for over twenty-five years. She has certain standards that she has set in all her classes and expects all students to obey them implicitly. Her students have come to know that not even a strand of hair must be out of place during Ms. Jones' sessions. This year however, for the first time in the school's fifteen-year history, a set of Grade Nine Education Students (GNES) have been sent to the school by the Ministry of Education (MoE). Every teacher complained about their apparent lack of ability to follow procedures and their below average performance. The principal, Mr.Walters, had assigned Ms. Jones as their teacher of math and home room teacher and she has been trying, albeit unsuccessfully to get them to conform and improve their grades.

One Thursday evening after a particularly frustrating session, Ms. Jones went to Mr.Jackson, the dean of discipline, for his assistance in dealing with the issue she was having with her class. On this particular day, after teaching for the first twenty minutes, she gave the students individual work to complete during the second half of the lesson, to allow time for her to conduct individual student conferences as they came with their books. However, this process was frequently interrupted as students kept asking questions and making off-task calling out. This resulted in the teacher being unable to give her undivided attention to the individual discussions. After several attempts to restore order and proceed with the class, she gave up in frustration. Ms. Jones then stormed out of the class, slammed the door and marched to the dean's office explaining that this kind of thing happened frequently with this class and she was becoming increasingly angry and ready to call it quits with the group. She also pointed out that her log book was filled with pages of complaints from other subject teachers about this class.

QUESTIONS FOR DISCUSSION:

8. What do you think the teacher could have done before, during and after this lesson to establish/reinforce her ground rules?

9. The fact that Ms. Jones walked out in frustration, what are the implications for the classroom organization?

10. Do you think Ms. Jones should involve other persons besides the dean in this situation? Discuss the reasons for your answer.

11. If you were Mr. Jackson, what advice would you give to Ms. Jones on how to avoid a recurrence of this situation?

12. Ms. Jones mentions that she has logged complaints from other teachers. Discuss how this can help or compound the situation.

13. The case mentions that this is the first set of GNES students. What is the implication of their behaviour/performance for subsequent groups?

14. What possible intervention strategies could the school implement to assist students and teachers?

CM #5:
Double Trouble With Bubble Gum

Mr. Miller, a senior teacher, was in the middle of his lesson with his grade 11 economics class. During the lesson, a student, Maria, kept blowing bubbles from the gum she was chewing, totally ignoring the fact that she was breaking two school rules: (1) Chewing gum is prohibited; (2) Do not cause disruption to the teaching/learning process. Despite being spoken to by the class monitor and the teacher repeatedly, Maria, who claimed not to have completed the homework because she did not understand a concept, continued to chew gum and make the annoying "pop" sounds as the bubbles she blew burst. Each time it happened, a few students sitting around her burst out in giggles.

Mr. Miller asked her once again to discard the gum and become a productive student in the class. She openly refused. After two more attempts, she still refused. The rest of the class watched with interest – taking the focus away from the lesson and directly onto his attempts to make this student comply. Exasperated, he asked her to leave the room. Again, she refused. Mr. Miller made a deliberate attempt to pack up his things, and asked the class to take up their things and follow him. He left the class, leaving behind the student in question. Even the girls who had been supporting her through their giggles hurriedly packed up and followed suit. Annoyed, Maria went to the vice-principal and told her that she was unable to follow the content of the lesson and when she expressed her inability to comprehend the subject matter, the teacher refused to give her any attention. The vice principal, Mrs. Susan Haye, summoned Mr. Miller. He explained that the student had been rude, defiant and disruptive and had refused to comply with his instructions. Since her actions were in direct contravention to the learning process, he resorted to taking the class to another room and so both he and them left the classroom.

QUESTIONS FOR DISCUSSION:

9. What should have been Mr. Miller's immediate course of action while he was still in the classroom?

10. Does Maria have a legitimate case?

11. What would you suggest as a long term strategy for preventing this kind of situation recurring with this student or any other student?

12. Who else may need to be involved in the situation? Why?

13. How appropriate was Mr. Miller's action of leaving the classroom with the rest of the students?

14. If you were the vice principal, how would you handle this case?

15. Is there anything in the Education Code of Regulations and/or Child Care Protection Act that addresses the issue(s) identified in the case?

16. Conduct a needs assessment to ascertain if there is need for any professional development training based on the issue(s) in the case.

CM #6:
Out Of Many One People

It has been just over two months since fourteen-year old twins Li Qiang and Liu Wei Yuen were transferred to New Hall High, a high school that boasted diversity. Mr. Griffiths, a veteran educator, has been having difficulties getting the boys to participate in his social studies class. The boys sit beside each other every day in the back of the room, despite Mr. Griffith's best efforts to get them closer to the front and more involved. In Mr. Griffith's eyes, the boys did not seem to be settling into the culture of his class. He tried persistently to engage them in discussions using trusted questioning techniques. However, as soon as either of them began to share, after a word or two they would stop. Interestingly, whenever Mr. Griffiths asked them to stay back and engaged them in oral questioning, they knew the answers to the questions discussed.

Another issue that existed was that every day as Mr. Griffiths took the register, there was always an orchestrated hush as he approached the Yuens' names. There was always an observable struggle with the correct pronunciation of the boys' names and having a slight stutter did not help. The other students always found this amusing and their response at times was to break out in gibberish. The last time this happened, Li Qiang and Liu Wei actually walked out of the class. They did not show up for class the next day, even though they were in school.

Mr. Griffiths took notice of the fact that during break and lunch periods the boys tended to be by themselves or could be seen in the company of three other Chinese-Jamaican students who also attended the school; one of whom was in a higher grade and the others in lower grades. Mr. Griffiths made a mental note to report this to the students' services clerk as this was not in keeping with the cultural immersion that formed a part of the school's culture. He also noted that part of the reason for this was the mockery of the foreign students' habits and he was committed to helping to stem this.

It was the end of a tiring day and Mr. Griffiths was being summoned to the office via the intercom. He headed to the principal's office where he saw the parents of Richard Matthews, one of his social studies students. Two days prior, Richard had been assigned a detention which his parents felt was not justifiable. Principal Aubrey asked Mr. Griffiths to explain the situation. He expressed that during his classes a part of the class activity was for each student to read a selected section of the textbook aloud. He indicated that when it was time for Li Qiang to read, in his evidently strong Chinese accent, he shook his head saying "I no go read". He did this repeatedly and tried to walk out. He explained that he intercepted him and informed him that if he didn't, he would not be released for lunch with the others. Subsequently Li Qiang attempted to read the paragraph he was assigned. He read slowly and mispronounced several of the words. It was at that point that Richard shouted out "I thought all Chiney was bright! Go learn fi read, or go sell patty or something". This outburst caused a loud uproar of laughter among the students. The laughter and Richard's persistence in jeering the twins angered Li

Qiang to the point where he got up and punched Richard. Mr. Griffiths pointed out that several students, including Richard and Li Qiang, were given detention.

QUESTIONS FOR DISCUSSION:

8. Identify some of the main issues in this case.

9. Would you agree that Mr. Griffiths made attempts to integrate the boys into the culture of his class? How did he do this?

10. Is he going about this integration the right way? How else would you advise Mr. Griffiths to handle this situation?

11. Are the Chinese nationals actions justified at anytime? Why/Why not?

12. How would you describe Mr. Griffiths' management of the classroom?

13. If you were the school's administrator, how would you assist the students of different cultures to integrate into the school community?

14. Is there anything in the Education Code of Regulations that addresses the issue(s) identified in the case?

15. Conduct a needs assessment to ascertain if there is need for any professional development training based on the issue(s) in the case.

CM #7:
Understanding Individuality

Shaka Jackson, a tall, strapping young giant of a boy with a deep, mahogany complexion has not gone unnoticed at Ernie Godfrey High. Everyone knows that he is a Maroon, a descendant of the Ashanti tribe. His parents are regular visitors to the school as they are often called in to help resolve one issue or another regarding Shaka. They are always clad in their traditional regalia which neither the average student nor teacher were accustomed to seeing. Because of this, their visits are usually accompanied by the ogle-eyed stares of the curious students. Shaka also draws attention to himself as he has been permitted to wear his beaded necklace to school and is the only boy in the school permitted to sport braided hair.

Shaka performs relatively well in school, even in non-academic areas. Last term Mrs. Morgan was satisfied with his participation in dance class. Her assessment of him was that he was not a fan of the compulsory dance class; however, he demonstrated competence in manipulating the basic elements of the genre that they explored.

This term however, Mrs. Morgan was becoming concerned because the second term's exploration of traditional cultural dance forms had excited everyone but Shaka. He had failed all the assignments on revivalism and was becoming increasingly defiant, and had refused to participate. The other students were not amused and now no one wanted to work with Shaka. This led to several arguments among the students. Just this morning Mrs. Morgan had to quell another when she spoke to Shaka:

Jessica: Miss run the boy out of the class. He's just killing the vibes!

Mrs. Morgan: Shaka, the work assigned is the work that is going be completed. All you are being asked to do is to give it a try. I am sure the others will work with you.

Mark: I'm not working with him. Because of him we almost fail last time. So put him in a next group Miss.

Erica: You better work with him. Next thing him obeah me. Maroon obeah strong.

The class erupts in laughter.

Shaka: Nobody can force me to do what I don't want to, or believe what they believe in.

Mrs. Morgan: Shaka, this is a school and we operate in a social setting. To do otherwise is to set up yourself for failure. I will talk to you after class but in the meantime, sit out the lesson for today and think on your actions.

After a while Mrs. Morgan was able to get the students to attend to the tasks assigned for the day. At the end of class she met with Shaka. She first apologized for the behaviour of the other students and tried to get him to explain his earlier behaviour. During their talk she learned that Shaka's religious beliefs did not allow him to participate freely in certain activities and while he was genuinely interested to learn about the Dinki Mini that was being explored, his religious beliefs did not permit him to dance with a member of the opposite sex, unless it was his life partner.

QUESTIONS FOR DISCUSSION:

12. What are the issues highlighted in this case?

13. What are some possible implications of these issues on students' learning?

14. Who are the other persons that may become involved in this situation? Why?

15. Examine Mrs. Morgan's response to Shaka's action.

16. How would you suggest Mrs. Morgan now proceed?

17. Is there anything in the Education Code of Regulations and/or Child Care Protection Act that address(es) the issue(s) identified in this case?

18. Based on the issues, what professional development initiative can you identify?

CM #8:
Let Them Run Loose

Charles Pearson has been a math teacher at Little Park High School for the past ten years. He has gained a reputation as the funky, fun teacher. Students like his classes because he is one of the few "cool adults".

It was Monday morning and the school had an unscheduled visit from its education officer. One of the classes he happened to attend was Mr. Pearson's class. When he arrived, Mr. Pearson was in the middle of a lesson and was working out a sum on the board. However, there was no order in the classroom. Some students were reading books; some were talking and laughing with one another; some even got up and left the classroom at random; only a few were participating. Mr. Pearson seemed oblivious to these things. The education officer stood by the classroom door and made a note of the scene before entering. Mr. Pearson was unaware of his presence until he realized that a hush had descended on the room. The education officer stepped in and sat at the back and for the remainder of the class, students paid attention and none walked out.

At the end of the lesson, he asked Mr. Pearson to remain behind to discuss the issue. Mr. Pearson admitted that the students would not listen despite the fact that he had repeatedly reminded them of the value of their education. He said he continued to teach so that those who were paying attention were not short changed in the process.

QUESTIONS FOR DISCUSSION:

7.   What are the main problems in Mr. Pearson's class?

8.   Why do you think these were happening?

9.   What is your opinion on Mr. Pearson's reputation as a "funky, fun, cool adult"?

10. What suggestions could you give to Mr. Pearson to improve his classroom management skills?

11. Was the education officer appropriate in her actions of bringing the class under control?

12. If you were the education officer, what would be your next course of action?

13. Is there anything in the Education Code of Regulations that addresses the issues identified in the case?

CM #9:
The Plot

The principal of New Direction Academy has a low tolerance for indiscipline having seen what it can do to educational institutions. When he was appointed to the position five years ago, he vowed to develop a vision that embraced the notion of high academic excellence and discipline. However, the school faces challenges based on the students it gets and the surrounding communities. Based on the regulations of the Ministry of Education, the school is not able to "hand-pick" the students listed on its register. In recent times too, the school has been struggling with an increase in incidences of school violence, drug abuse, petty theft and extortion. The principal has involved the Ministry of Education and now feels he has exhausted the limited resources at the school. The deans of discipline appear ineffective and the guidance counsellors are overwhelmed by the complexities of the students' needs. They fear these students grapple with emotional and behavioural disorders they are not equipped to handle at the school. Also, the parents feel defeated but often do not want their child to be labelled or asked to leave the school.

The school has had many battles with the Ministry of Education over students that they have tried to expel and were bombarded about the paucity of data presented to substantiate the request for expulsions.

Last month, following a particular disturbing incident, the principal decided to suspend a student and refer the incident to the board. The board's disciplinary committee met and took the decision to expel the student. The parent, Mrs. Buckle, was surprised when she was summoned to the school and issued a letter informing her that she will need to make arrangements for her son Mario to continue his education elsewhere. Mario, a third former, had only just returned from a five-day suspension for throwing a rock and breaking a window of the principal's car. Mrs. Buckle agreed that Mario can be mischievous but felt the administration's decision was strange and stringent. As far as she knew his action was a one-time infraction. After all, Mario has maintained a B+ average for the past three years.

Failing to get the school to relent and reverse its decision, she brought the matter to the Ministry of Education who favoured her stance on the matter. The school's education officer visited the school to have a meeting regarding the issue but found that Mario's actions over the years amounted to more than an "one time infraction".   Mario's record included:

- Phone calls to the parents from the form teacher regarding lateness for classes and skipping class
- Class disruptions
- Several involvement in fights
- Allegations of theft and extortion
- Insubordination and disrespect to staff
- Willfully damaging school property
- Suspicion of smoking marijuana
- A photocopy of a page from one of his books with a note that says he would shoot a teacher if he had a gun

These records were provided only because the EO was given the mandate by the regional director of the MoE to revert the decision of the school. With all of this evidence however, it was easy to see why the school had taken the decision it had. Despite this however, the board was asked to rescind its decision of expulsion and give Mario additional days suspension because the evidence had not been previously shared with his parents, yet it had been on his personal file.

To prevent a repeat, the principal insisted that teachers, grade coordinators, counsellors and deans of disciplines keep thorough records of students' behaviour no matter how minor and ensure that these are communicated in writing to her so that she in turn can inform the parents.

QUESTIONS FOR DISCUSSION:

1. Was the school justified in asking Mario's mom to withdraw him from the school?

2. What are some possible reasons Mario's mom is shocked by the list of misdemeanors?

3. How can a lack of adequate documentation and record-keeping issues at the school become problematic?

4. Mario's mom was not informed about most of his misdemeanors. What does that say about the school's policy of collaboration with parents?

5. Do you think the school employed enough intervention strategies to help Mario?

6. Was the parent right in taking the matter to the Ministry of Education?

7. Is there anything in the Education Code of Regulations and/or Child Care Protection Act that addresses the issue(s) present in this case?

8. Conduct a needs assessment to ascertain if there is need for any professional development training based on the issue(s) in the case.

CM #10:
Lack of Interest in Learning?

Danny attends Middleton Primary School and is currently in grade 5. His father resides overseas and he lives in Jamaica with his mother. At the beginning of every school year, Danny would turn out to school with all his required resources and his correct uniform. By the end of September, he would lose all his books and his uniform would be torn and stained. This has been the trend with Danny from grade 3.

Now in grade 5, he is in Ms. Cunningham's class. Ms. Cunningham is one of the stalwarts of the school and she is a champion for the cause of education. She noted that the routine of starting the school year with the relevant material continued. By the third week in September, Danny had only two books and his uniform was torn and covered in stains. Ms. Cunningham had found the other books laying around in the classroom and had stored them in her drawer. Because of his actions, when he was in class and given work, Danny was the first to complain that he didn't have any books and accused his classmates of stealing them. Ms. Cunningham would then produce the book required for him to do his work. This angered him and defeated his purpose so he would some-times tear the page from the book. Ms. Cunningham was also aware of this and would watch him keenly to prevent this from happening. She would take the book from him after class for safe keeping.

Danny had got very rowdy and sometimes, deliberately provoked other students to start a fight so he would be sent out of the class. On the third occasion, Ms. Cunningham picked up on this strategy and placed him to sit at her desk.

Ms. Cunningham tried to get his parents more involved in his learning but she noticed that when his mother is contacted, she doesn't respond. However, his father would occasionally contact the school from overseas. The father had also provided his contact information so the school may reach him easily. When a complaint is made to him, Danny's behaviour would improve for a while but shortly thereafter, he would revert to his old ways. Ms. Cunningham reported the matter to the guidance counsellor who has offered counselling to Danny and recommends that he be tested for attention deficit disorder (ADD) and this has yet to be done. She has also scheduled a home visit.

QUESTIONS FOR DISCUSSION:

16. Discuss the course of action taken by Ms. Cunningham to assist Danny.

17. Do you think the parenting structure has an impact on Danny's behaviour? How so?

18. Do you think Ms. Cunningham's method of handling the situation is appropriate and/or effective? Why/why not?

19. Who are the other individuals who may possibly get involved in this situation?

20. Is there anything in the Education Code of Regulations and/or Child Care Protection Act that addresses the issue(s) identified in the case?

CM#11:
Mr. Technological Gadget

Teacher James teaches grade 3k. He is very fascinated with technology and would often use it in some of his lessons. The students enjoy when he uses this to enhance his lessons. However, Teacher James sometimes misuses technology in class. He would often answer his cell phone during class, pause his lessons, and go outside for lengthy conversations leaving the students unmonitored. During these intervals, the students would become noisy, and disrupt nearby classes. The other teachers would complain. Some students have informed their parents about this action, and some of the parents have made complaints to the principal, yet still the practice persists.

One day, the period just before lunch, Teacher James was doing a math lesson. He then gave the students a few math problems to solve in pairs. He then sat at his desk, took out his cell phone and began texting. Ten minutes later, there was a scream and a loud commotion in the middle of the room. When he went to investigate, there was a student with blood streaming down the side of his face. Teacher James had no clue as to what happened.

QUESTIONS FOR DISCUSSION

1. Identify the issues in the case, and can you assess them against the Education Code of Regulations or Child Care and Protection Act?
2. Does Teacher James' actions conflict with the ICT policies of the institution or national ICT policies?
3. Examine Teacher James' actions. How do you think they impacted the teaching and learning process?
4. Discuss the professionalism of the characters in the scenario.
5. What should be the next step in the scenario?
6. Can you identify the need for a professional development initiative? If yes, what would it be about?

CM# 12:
The Confrontation

June's favourite subjects are visual art and English literature. She is particularly fond of art because Mr. Jack the art teacher, helped her two years ago to discover she had skills to become a graphic artist if she desires to.

One day, during literature session, Ms. Black, the teacher, gave the class pair work. As they sat working Mr. Jack walked by the classroom. Shortly after his departure, Ms. Black commented with a chuckle: "Lawd, Missa Jack nuh si dat him need a new pair of shoes. Mi affi go tease him later when we meet up." Some students giggled. One student who lived in the same community as Mr. Jack was sitting close to Ms. Black's desk. The student started talking about him. Ms. Black joined the conversation and several unkind and personal things were discussed about him and his family, much to the annoyance of June who was sitting close enough to hear them. "Miss I am trying to concentrate and you are disturbing me," uttered Melissa who was sitting beside and working with June, in a clipped tone. Ms. Black was startled and reprimanded Melissa for her tone.

Melissa: Maybe if you were not disturbing me, I wouldn't have to use this tone.

Ms. Black: Who are you addressing like that? Do I look like one of your classmates?

Melissa: Well you are surely acting like one.

Ms. Black: Excuse me? You are very disrespectful. You will receive a demerit for your insolence.

Melissa: And the ministry should fire yuh. Betta yuh just stop talk yah Miss and let mi get fi finish mi work in peace. If not, mek mi know so mi can go outside go find supm fi do. (She hissed her teeth.)

Ms. Black: Oh, so I am not allowed to speak in my own classroom? You know what, after class, I am taking you to the dean of discipline's office.

Melissa: Oh no, do not wait until after class. Let's go now. (She angrily grabbed her backpack, stuffed her things in it and held it to her chest, stood and stared at Ms. Black.)

Miss Black: (Standing and pointing towards the door.) Get out of my class! You will not stay inside here and speak to me like that. Out! I will deal with you after class.

(Melissa walked to the door then turned.)

Melissa: I am going to the vice principal. Hope you can tell her all you said about Mr. Jack earlier.

June: I am coming with you Melissa because you will need a witness. I don't know why some teachers think it is okay to chat other teachers…and with students at that. (She packed her things. Both Melissa and June then disappeared through the door.)

Ms. Black could hardly conceal her embarrassment as the rest of the class looked on silently. She awkwardly told them to continue working. She sat in her chair and hung her head in her hand.

QUESTIONS FOR DISCUSSION

1. What are the main issues in the case?

2. How would you assess Melissa's and June's actions?

3. What conclusions can you draw about Ms. Black's relationship with her students and the impact it has on her professionalism?

4. How do you think Ms. Black could have handled the situation for a different outcome?

5. Can you identify the need for any professional development initiative? What would it be?

6. Is there anything in the Education Code of Regulations that addresses the issues identified in the case?

ADMINISTRATIVE MANAGEMENT

Administrative Management Has its Principles

The administrator in any school usually has his plate full. Of what you may ask, so here goes: staff to attend to, parents wanting to be heard, papers to shuffle, disciplinary actions to decide on, board personnel to meet, class visits to make, meetings to attend and a myriad of other tasks too numerous to mention. Consequently, a school's success depends on how effective administrators are in finding the balance between people and production. Remember earlier in this text I stated that the "teaching profession is a whole conglomerate by itself"? So yes! Production.

There is no single answer one could give if one were to be asked about the best approach to school administration as what works in one situation may not work elsewhere, and what works with one group may not do so well with another. We however know that there are some principles to always bear in mind when functioning in an administrative capacity. Let us look at some principles that administrators must seek to maintain:

1. Balance between people's concern and production goals

People – staff, students, parents – need to be assured that the administrator cares about their well-being. Without this attitude of care, people may not cooperate or go beyond the call of duty. A school's vision and mission may not be attained if the institution's leaders do not care for the concerns of the persons in the school.

Equally though, administrators must always keep the productivity goal in mind as this is just as important. The school's administrator has to check the data re exam results, must perform class quality assurance checks, and do all that indicates that the school is an entity that must produce. Schools are judged on their level of productivity as measured in the pass rates in external examinations and the accomplishment of targets outlined in their five-year plan or School Improvement Plan (SIP). The role of middle managers is crucial to this process, hence, school supervisors are duty bound to be production supervisors. Administrators cannot achieve this success on their own. It is prudent that they utilize the principle of …

2. Collaboration and cooperation

The modern educational leader cannot escape the matter of collaboration and cooperation. The modern administrative manager has to be open to working collaboratively with others, sharing of himself/herself and learning from what others have to offer. He/she has to build a network. Cooperation and collaboration are essential if educational leaders are to benefit from the human resources around them. By becoming engaged in collaboration and seeking cooperation, the educational administrator encourages broad-based participation that will build a cohesive team rather than a set of individuals. Collaboration and cooperation often indicate that staff members understand the goals of the institution. With collaboration and cooperation in full effect, it certainly leads to staff feeling a sense of…

3. Empowerment

No school administrator is independent – not within the school nor the school district; rather all should be interdependent. It is this knowledge of interdependency that will be used to achieve collective goals and create a sense of belonging and ownership. This will lead to an enhancement of feeling of self-efficacy among organizational members. Leaders who empower their employees pull them rather than push them towards the goal or vision of the institution. Even in handling various situations, administrators must be cognizant of how decisions affect individuals and their implication for the organization. Although there is no blueprint for dealing with situations, administrators must be empowered to do the right thing, and thus will empower their staff likewise. Each leader must always bear in mind that his/her situation demands that unique and creative response.

This section gives some insightful experiences from the perspectives of various administrators and how they dealt with the situations. Please be sure to make note of the principles mentioned and not mentioned.

Dorraine Reid
Liston Aiken

AM #1:
Jane Returns Early Pt. 2
(See Case 1 In Behavior Mgmt)

Jane Doherty had an altercation with Mr. Brown when she walked into his class without permission and was blatantly rude to him. The school's administration interpreted her behaviour as rude and disrespectful. Consequently, Jane was suspended for a period of five school days.

On the fourth day, Jane showed up at school to attend a field trip to the annual theatre Jamboree. Ms. Ross, Jane's form teacher, reported this to the school's administrator who checked her file to verify if she was eligible for school. During the gathering in the school hall, Ms. Ross called Jane. When questioned by Ms. Ross about her legitimacy on the school's compound, she explained that one of the three school's administrators (Ms. Campbell) told her to return on the fifth day of the month. Mr. Brown saw Ms. Ross conversing with Jane and became very upset that she was allowed back in school. He asked Ms. Ross why the student was on the school's compound when she was supposed to be on suspension. Ms. Ross tried to explain what had happened and her intention to handle the situation, but an angry Mr. Brown would not give her the chance to do so and would cut her off with an argument of his own. He eventually stormed away leaving Ms. Ross standing in the middle of the school's main hall. Ms. Ross then made her way to the office where she saw Mr. Brown. She told him in no uncertain terms what she thought about his actions. A heated argument developed but was quickly squashed by the vice principal.

QUESTIONS FOR DISCUSSION:

1. Should Jane be allowed to attend the field trip?

2. Is Ms. Ross justified in making the report to the school's administrators of Jane's early return?

3. On the fifth day when Jane returns to school, if you were Ms. Ross, what would you do?

4. As the school's administrator, how would you respond to Mr. Brown?

5. Was Mr. Brown justified in his behaviour?

6. As a school's administrator, if Mr. Brown was a first time teacher and this happened, how would you respond? If he were a teacher with three or more years of experience, would you respond differently?

7. Is there anything in the Education Code of Regulation that addresses the issue(s) identified in the case?

8. Conduct a needs assessment to ascertain if there is need for any professional development training based on the issue(s) in the case.

AM #2:
....And They Got Physical

Mr. John Dixon, a senior teacher, was walking the school's compound when he saw a group of girls gathered behind the ancillary building at the stand pipe. He called to the young ladies and instructed them to get to their classes. At the sound of his voice, some ran but a few remained. Mr. Dixon went up to the girls:

Mr. Dixon: Young ladies, turn off the pipe and get to your classes.

Girl 1: Sir we are going. Just waiting on Sarah.

Mr. Dixon: None of you should be at the pipe at this time. You should all be in your classes.

Sarah:	Me a wash me face (*she proceeds to wash her hands*).
Mr. Dixon:	Excuse me? All of you, leave this area for your class immediately. (*Girl one starts to move. Sarah continues washing her hands. The others look on.*)

Mr. Dixon then attempted to turn the pipe off. As he did this Sarah held on to the faucet. He tried to pry her hands away and a tussle developed between the two. Sarah slapped Mr. Dixon in the face. He let go off the faucet and grabbed her by the shoulders and shook her. Sarah responded with more blows. Students who were looking on screamed and this alerted others. A male ancillary worker who was in the vicinity stepped in and broke up the squabble. Shortly after, the dean of discipline arrived. Sarah and the other girls were taken to the principal's office. Both Sarah and Mr. Dixon were asked to write reports on the incident and present these to the principal.

The following day, the school's disciplinary committee met and the girls were placed in detention for skipping classes. Sarah was however pulled from classes for two days and placed on in-house suspension. Those days were spent in the principal's office to allow her to reflect on her actions. The committee also took the decision to give her the maximum suspension of ten days (10 days) after which she was to return to school with her parents, wearing black and white attire instead of the normal school uniform. The case was also referred to the board for a disciplinary hearing.

After the personnel committee of the board met, Sarah was allowed to return to school and resume regular classes. The staff was angry as they thought the student's actions warranted an expulsion. They staged a sit-in for two days.

QUESTIONS FOR DISCUSSION:

9. Outline the various issues in this case.

10. Did Mr. Dixon act appropriately when he saw the girls at the pipe?

11. Discuss the response of the students to Mr. Dixon.

12. Suggest alternative approaches that could have been employed to prevent the incident from escalating.

13. Do you believe the series of actions taken by the principal were reasonable?

14. Was Sarah punished twice? Why/Why not?

15. How can this affect the results if the parents decide to pursue the matter legally?

16. How would you advise the principal in this matter?

17. Why do you believe the student was not expelled?

18. Do you agree with the action of the staff? Justify your response.

19. Is there anything in the Education Code of Regulation/Child Care Protection Act that addresses the issue(s) identified in the case?

20. Conduct a needs assessment to ascertain if there is need for any professional development training based on the issue(s) in the case.

AM #3:
Throw Them Away

It is the second week in July and the academic school year has ended. Most of the teachers of the Grandshire High School have neatly and safely packed away their resources for the summer holiday, while others were participating in the school's annual summer class activities. The final week in July, the remaining teachers packed their resources away in the usual manner and left the school compound.

Unknown to the teachers, Principal Mary Robinson had decided to refurbish the staffroom to include cubicles that would now see each teacher with a definitive personal space. The workmen were instructed to remove everything from the staffroom and place them outside to facilitate completion of the tasks.

The new school year started as usual in September. Teachers turned up to work to find all their possessions outside, exposed to the natural elements. Tempers flared. Some persons were unable to locate any of their possessions. As teachers went to the cubicles erected in the spaces where their desks used to be, some found they were displaced as the cubicles made the space smaller. Again, tempers flared even more.

Among those displaced were the two drama teachers. During that first week while other teachers were trying to get settled, Ms. Riley was unable to remove her things as the space being worked on to house herself and Mr. Duncan was not yet ready. Their resources had to remain outside.

At the beginning of the second week, teaching was in full gear. The new space for Ms. Riley and Mr. Duncan was also finished but their possessions could not be found. Ms. Riley located her desk and chair but all her resources (books, files, CDs, DVDs) were missing. She spoke with her supervisor about the matter who in turn spoke to the grounds men. The grounds men indicated that at the end of the first week of school, they had been instructed to throw away everything that was remaining on the outside as teachers had one week to settle into their new spaces.

Ms. Riley reported the matter to the vice principal who attempted to get the grounds men to go back into the rubble that were not yet disposed of to retrieve Ms. Riley's possessions. None of them complied. Ms. Riley attempted to speak with the principal on the matter but her request for the meeting was denied. By mid week she was very frustrated as she was unable to teach as she had no material. The principal continued to refuse her request for a meeting. Upon realizing that the principal would not address her situation, Ms. Riley went and repurchased a few texts so she could start teaching. Tension developed between Ms. Riley and the principal. Ms. Riley dropped all the activities in which she was involved and only did the minimum required of her as a classroom teacher. This affected the staff as she was very efficient, highly successful and very involved. Staff morale became low. No one spoke openly about it but everyone was concerned about the apparent lack of respect displayed. It made the vice principal in charge of staff affairs very concerned as she knew the prolonged period of this could seriously affect the teachers' and students' performance.

QUESTIONS FOR DISCUSSION:

19. Discuss the actions of the principal focusing on appropriateness and leadership style.

20. Discuss the teachers' reaction to the refurbishing and the effect it had on them?

21. How could this have been avoided?

22. From a professional and personal perspective, how would you advise Ms. Riley to proceed?

23. Discuss the response of the grounds men to the vice principal's request focusing on chain of command, leadership and sanctions, etc.

24. Based on the issue(s) highlighted, do you see the need for a professional development seminar? What would it be about?

25. Is there anything in the Education Code of Regulation that addresses the issue(s) identified in this case?

AM #4:
Study Leave 'Denied'

It was September, 2012. Maria Rowe was in her tenth year of teaching. Nine and a half of those years have been spent at Fair Town High School where she is currently a grade 11 form teacher and teaches music to grade 7 to 11 students. At the beginning of the academic year, Ms. Rowe applied for one year study leave along with eight months vacation leave effective September 2013. She indicated in her application letter that her two previous applications for vacation leave were denied. The current leave application was recommended by the school board and sent to the Ministry of Education for approval.

Ms. Rowe later wrote a letter requesting a deferral of the study leave to the following year but indicated she would take up the vacation leave. As the summer break approached, Ms. Rowe noted that she did not receive a response from the Ministry of Education. She enquired frequently about her status from the principal and was told nothing was forthcoming from the Ministry of Education. Towards the end of the summer holiday, Ms. Rowe visited the personnel department at the ministry and was told that her name had been removed from the list since she had deferred the leave. She explained it was the study leave component she had deferred and produced her letter as evidence of this. She went back to her principal who apologized and admitted she had erred. She explained that when she received the letter requesting the deferral of study leave, she had not absorbed the section that spoke about her intention to take up the vacation leave, hence her name had not been sent to the MoE. Instead the VP replaced it with that of another teacher whose study leave was initially denied. Therefore, the ministry had no record of Ms. Rowe's request to go on leave the following school year.

QUESTIONS FOR DISCUSSION:

21. What are some of the issues in this case?

22. Should Ms. Rowe's leave request be given consideration?

23. Did the principal act appropriately?

24. What steps can Ms. Rowe take to address this situation?

25. Is there anything in the Education Code of Regulation that addresses the issue(s) identified in this case?

AM #5:
The Missing Cell Phone

Mr. Millwood had a group of five students in his office, just before the lunch period, discussing the assignment that was due in the next four days. During this time, his personal items including his Samsung cell phone were scattered on his desk. When the lunch bell went, he dismissed the students promptly as he was scheduled to monitor lunch lines for the first 20 minutes in the cafeteria. When the students left, he quickly secured the working handouts and locked the door behind him. As he locked the door, he remembered he had not taken up his cell phone but decided against re-opening and turning back since he'd be back in less than half an hour.

At the end of his shift, he returned to his office to retrieve his cell phone but it was missing from his desk. After searching his office for 10-15 minutes and not finding it, he went in search of the five students who had been in his office.

The students denied taking the phone and were released. He reported the situation to the principal. The following day, Principal Watson called the students to her office and questioned them based on Mr. Millwood's story. They once again denied the allegation.

Four days later there was a fracas on the school's compound involving two girls and a boy. The students were taken by the dean of discipline to the principal's office. Principal Watson inquired the reason for the fracas and it was revealed that the girls had given the boy a phone to unlock. He was then supposed to get it sold and a percentage of the money was to be given to them. However, the boy, Tommy, did not give them the agreed amount. He then revealed that it was Mr. Millwood's cell phone. The girls had stolen the phone, given it to him to unlock and he had given it to Marcus (the student council representative) to sell. He further explained that they were unable to sell it for the price they had agreed on, hence the money was short.

Principal Watson reprimanded the girls strongly as they had lied about not taking the phone. Marcus was immediately summoned to the principal's office and reprimanded for the role he played in the incident. In his defence, Marcus explained that he figured the phone was stolen but he didn't know it was from Mr. Millwood. He further explained that this was not the first time he was selling a phone for Tommy because that was how their business was designed. Tommy does the unlocking and he does the selling. The two girls and Tommy were given five days suspension for stealing the phone and knowingly accepting and agreeing to sell stolen property, while Marcus was given ten days for knowingly accepting and selling stolen property. The students' parents were informed and told to return to school with them at the end of their suspension.

QUESTIONS FOR DISCUSSION:

15. Identify the issues in this case?

16. Was Mr. Millwood justified in his actions when he called in the students as suspects about the missing phone?

17. If you were Mr. Millwood, is there anything you would have done differently? Explain.

18. Do you believe the sanctions given to the students were fair? Why?

19. Should Marcus retain his student leadership position?

20. What strategies would you employ going forward?

21. Is there anything in the Education Code of Regulation that addresses the issue(s) identified in the case?

AM #6:
Mutual Benefits

It is the peak of the schoolboy football season and for the first time in the school's history the Da'Costa Cup team actually has a chance to make it to the finals. However, rumours were being circulated that a female teacher was involved in a less than professional relationship with a male student, a key player on this celebrated team. Before long the rumours reached the ears of the acting principal, who immediately launched an investigation into the matter. While no tangible evidence was found, the allegations had some merit based on the students' admission.

The teacher in question had been making great strides in a department that had been suffering over the past three years. A veteran teacher who had guided the students and school to great successes at the Caribbean Secondary Examination (CSEC) level had died in tragic circumstances. Since then, three teachers had been employed to fill the role but had various shortcomings. Of the lot, the current teacher, the one in question, seemed the most promising; importantly, the students loved her and enjoyed her teaching styles. The acting principal, in considering the scores of students preparing to sit the subject in the upcoming CSEC exams, almost the entire graduating class, opted to issue the teacher with a letter of reprimand, cautioning her against any questionable involvement with the student. It would seem however, that this was not enough to quell the rumours.

Before long, their involvement became undeniable even to the unconcerned. The administration undoubtedly had to inform the student's parents of what they had learned. At this point, the seventeen-year old student threatened to run away from home and possibly commit suicide if he was prevented from speaking with the teacher or if her position at the school was terminated. There were numerous consultations with the mother who was more than fearful for her son's well-being. He was temporarily withdrawn from school but was anxious to return with final exams approaching, and seeing that the peak of the football season was imminent.

Before long, the mother informed the school that she had accepted the relationship and wished for her son to return to school. The administration decided to allow the student to complete the year but he would not be eligible for their sixth form programme. The teacher would not be relieved of her duties so as not to jeopardize the projected successes in the CSEC examinations. However, she would not be permitted to have direct contact with the student on campus or while he was in his uniform.

QUESTIONS FOR DISCUSSION:

21. Identify the series of actions taken by the acting principal? Were they appropriate?

22. What are the issues outlined in this case?

23. Do you believe the final decision was appropriate?

24. How do you think this could affect staff morale?

25. What is the role of the school board in this situation?

26. Are there other persons who could become involved in this situation?

27. Discuss the compromise reached.

28. What steps would you have taken in this situation were you the acting principal?

29. Explain whether there is need for a professional development seminar based on the issues identified in this case.

30. Is there anything in the Education Code of Regulation/Child Care and Protection Act that speaks to the issue(s) identified in the case?

AM #7:
No Escaping The Past

It was just before the start of the final semester of Andrea's undergraduate studies. She desired nothing more than walking across the stage to collect her Bachelor of Arts in Education degree and continuing the quest to help educate the nation's youth. One week before school began, Andrea was asked to attend a meeting with the dean of academic affairs. She was anxious to learn what the meeting was about. On her way she wondered if she had won a national award as she knew she had been doing exceptionally well. She had an almost perfect GPA and the respect of her lecturers.

When she got to the office, both the dean and the principal were waiting. A dread filled her lower abdomen as she listened to the principal who revealed that it had been brought to his attention that while she was in high school she had been expelled because of a video that had gone viral of her engaging in a sexual act. Andrea was shocked but did not deny the frustrating experience that occurred six and a half years ago. The principal revealed that one of her colleagues brought it to his attention and showed him the video that was on the Internet. Andrea was asked not to return for her final semester.

QUESTIONS FOR DISCUSSION:

17. On what grounds would the principal make such a decision?

18. Do you believe his decision was justified? Explain.

19. What course of action do you believe the principal should have taken?

20. What steps should Andrea take?

21. Is there anything in the Education Code of Regulation that addresses the issue(s) in this case?

AM #8:
The 'Grass' Cookies

Angels High School for Girls is a very prominent high school whose students are children whose parents belong to the upper echelons of society. These students are exceptionally wealthy but they are also extremely high achievers. As a Catholic institution, the girls are expected to follow the Christian principles of the institution and deviation in any form is completely unacceptable. The school's principal, Sister Mary Wisdom, is proud of the fifty-year legacy and its immaculate reputation.

It was Sports Day and at the annual event, Elizabeth, one of the school's brightest students, after running the 100m sprint race, went to her house boothe and collapsed in the arms of Ms. Riley, the House Mother. She was rushed to the nurse's station. The nurse observed that her heart was beating faster than its normal pace but there were no other obvious signs of distress. The nurse asked the students who took her to lay her in the bed and leave her. After Elizabeth revived, the nurse asked her about her activities before the race. Elizabeth looked sheepish and remained silent. The nurse bluntly inquired if she smoked marijuana. Elizabeth, cognizant of the Christian principles of the school, said no. She however admitted to the nurse that shortly before she ran the 100m sprints, she consumed two cookies laced with marijuana. She went on to reveal that she got it from a grade 11 student and that she was not the only one who had eaten the cookie. A shocked Ms. Riley questioned Elizabeth further and instructed her to write down the names of all the students who were involved in the baking and distribution of the cookies.

Ms. Riley then went in search of the girls and took them to the principal's office. Upon hearing Ms. Riley's report, Sister Mary Wisdom inquired of the girls if they had any more of the illegal substance on the compound. She instructed her secretary to call the police if any of the substance was found. Their belongings were searched in their presence. When Sister Mary Wisdom was satisfied that the girls did not have any of the substance, nor did they have any of the cookies remaining, their parents were called in. The five girls who were involved were suspended for ten days. Upon their return to school, they had to make a presentation to the school about the consequences of using marijuana. They were struck from the graduation list. Three of the girls, Elizabeth included, were told that they could attend sixth form as they were 'A' students and first time offenders. The other two were not given that option as they had a track record for committing varying infractions.

QUESTIONS FOR DISCUSSION:

16. What are the issues in this situation?
17. If you were Ms. Riley, would you have taken the same course of action when the student revealed the information about the cookies?
18. Outline the principal's actions. Do you think she acted appropriately?
19. Was the punishment meted out to the girls reasonable?
20. Would you say there is any favouritism in the punishment meted out?
21. Are there any actions you think the principal should have taken that were not done?
22. Is there anything in the Education Code of Regulation/Child Care and Protection Act that addresses the issue(s) identified in the case?

AM #9:
Triple Threat

Bryan is a grade 11 student of the Gateway High School and is facing possible expulsion.

He became well known to the school's populace during the 8th grade when he got into a yard brawl. He had attacked several other boys with a chair, an incident that had disrupted the entire school. He had been suspended by the school's administration, received counselling and his parents were called in. Only his mother had come to the meeting with the school's administration. Incidentally, she had been on the compound the day the incident happened and blamed the other students for provoking her son.

When Bryan got to grade 9, he was again at the centre of another major conflict. Then he had been involved in a fracas in the town's square with students from the Bed Rock High School. On this day, he had stolen a knife from the Home Economics Centre before leaving school. A student had been injured in the fracas. His mom was called to the scene where she too became involved in the fracas and complained that her son had been provoked.

The incident created a heightened tension between both institutions. The following day, students from Bed Rock High School went to Gateway High School where Bryan attended, to attack students as a reprisal. Both institutions ended prematurely that day and remained closed the following day. The Ministry o   f Education was informed about the incident. Both schools' administration met along with the school resource officer (a member of the police force) to decide the way forward. It was decided that the students involved in the incident were to be removed from the institutions. Bed Rock High School's administration did that but at Gateway High, Bryan and his cronies were retained. Instead, they were suspended for ten days and their cases referred to the personnel of the school board. After the ten days, they were reinstated and given a strong warning. Before long, Bryan was labelled the school's don by both teachers and students. Some students even thought teachers were afraid of him. He attracted several young boys to his company and started a gang movement. It was also rumoured that he did violent things in the bus park and was involved in an inner city community gang.

Now in grade 11, Bryan was called to defend one of his cronies who felt he was disrespected by a student in a lower grade. Bryan went in search of the student and proceeded to inflict blows to his face without asking questions. This caused a major disruption in the school. During the disruption, he was given a knife by another student but after the fracas was quelled, he denied having the knife when he was asked by the school's vice principal. By this time school was dismissed, but the disruption was so widespread that the administration had to employ emergency strategies by locking the gate to prevent an escalation of the situation to the street. Students were ushered to their classrooms under the supervision of their form teachers. The police was also called in but they took long to get to the school. When they eventually came, they suggested that the matter be dealt with internally. The guidance counsellor and other teachers got involved. Bryan was taken to the office of the VP and was told he was going to be suspended and brought before the board. At mention of the board, he stormed out of the office and slammed the door. He was spoken to by a group of girls and he eventually went back to the VP's office.

On his return the VP inquired about his current behaviour…

VP: Bryan, why are you behaving like this?

Bryan: How mi a behave sir?

VP: Like how you did this afternoon and just now. You are behaving like a bad man. A don. Why?

Bryan: Mi not behaving like bad man. Mi is a bad man. Is just because mi respect you. But mi can do you things enuh.

VP: Do me things?

Bryan: Yes! Mi can do you things. Just like how you have power, I have power too.

The VP gave a letter to Bryan to take home. The VP then called his mother. The mother then complained to the VP that her son was always being provoked and that she heard that boys were on the street waiting for him. She was advised to pick him up herself.

The personnel committee of the school board notified Bryan and his parents of the hearing involving Bryan. Two weeks later, the meeting was convened to discuss the incident and the board made the decision to have him dismissed because they felt his 'don-ship' couldn't be accommodated by the school. This time both his mother and father came to the board meeting. The board explained that he was being dismissed as he was a repeat offender who caused the school to be locked down more than once, had threatened the vice principal and was a threat to other students. His father expressed shock and explained that he was not aware of the two previous incidents, nor any other infraction.

QUESTIONS FOR DISCUSSION:

14. Should stronger remedial measures have been taken for his first major offense?
15. What actions of the teachers did the students see that caused them to think that the teachers were afraid?
16. Should he have been removed from the school after the second incident?
17. Should he have been given a warning?
18. How much did the mother contribute towards the child's negative behaviour?
19. Discuss the role of the father in Bryan's life.
20. Is there anything in the Education Code of regulation/Child Care and Protection Act that will address the issue(s) identified in the case?
21. Conduct a needs assessment to ascertain if there is need for any professional development training based on the issue(s) in the case.

AM #10:
When You Go to Rome, Do as the Romans Do

Maya Allen is in grade 2 at Southfield Primary School. She was born in the

United States of America to a Jamaican mother and a US citizen father. The mother took the decision that they wanted her to have her primary education in Jamaica, so they moved to the southern side of the country famous for returning residents.

Maya was a disruptive child who had a short attention span and found it difficult to sit still and listen. She would constantly get up from her seat and move around the classroom. She would sometimes call to other students across the classroom and disrupt the teaching process. Even when she was spoken to by the teacher she wouldn't listen.

On this particular occasion, Maya ran to the back of the class to whisper in Jenny's ears while class was in progress. A frustrated Ms. Black slapped her on the hand and told her to have a seat. A shocked Maya stared at her for an interminable second before she sat. Ms. Black then continued her class. Maya sat, pouted and refused to do the work placed on the board. As the lesson progressed, Ms. Black was using the ruler to draw a triangle on the board when Maya shoved passed her, bounced her and the ruler fell and hit her. She cried out and stomped out of the class. She went home and reported to her parents that she was spanked twice by the teacher.

The following day Maya's mom (Pricilla) visited the school and went straight to Ms. Black's class.

Pricilla: Excuse me Miss, I would like to have a word with you.

Ms. Black: Did you make an appointment?

Pricilla: I don't need to make any appointment for this. You spanked my child twice and I am not happy about it.

Ms. Black: Mommy, if you did not make an appointment then you should report to the office. Besides, parents are not allowed to visit classrooms without administrative permission. Did you get a pass from the office clerk?

Pricilla: I'm here already. How dare you hit my child? Do you know who I am? You have absolutely no right.

Ms. Black: Miss, I did not spank— *(Pricilla cuts her off)*

Pricilla: This is Uncle Sam's child. She is not Jamaican. I can call them on you.

Ms. Black: Ma'am— (*She is cut off again*)

Pricilla: I will not have it. I didn't send my child here for you to beat. You need to go and have your own if you so well want somebody to beat.

Ms. Black: Well ma'am, since you do not want to listen to me, you will have to take this matter to the office. I need to get back to my class. (*She closes the door*)

This action by Ms. Black made Pricilla even more furious. She cursed loudly and her tirade was laced with several expletives. This attracted the attention of teachers who were in close proximity. They came outside to see what was happening. The security was called to escort Pricilla from the compound. She returned to the school the following day to speak with the principal who told her in no uncertain terms that if she continued to come to the school to abuse the teachers, she would be asked to withdraw her child from the school. She did not like that comment and decided she would be taking the matter to the Ministry of Education.

QUESTIONS FOR DISCUSSION:

9. Discuss the action of the teacher towards the child and assess for appropriateness.

10. What possible methods could the teacher have employed to reach Maya before resorting to slapping her?

11. Did the teacher respond appropriately to the parent?

12. Is there anything else Ms. Black could have done?

13. Was the principal justified in his comment to the parent?

14. What can you infer about the structure/system of this school?

15. How can the mother's response exacerbate the situation?

16. Is there anything in the Education Code of Regulation/Child Care and Protection Act that addresses the issue(s) identified in the case?

AM #11:
In This Department

Ms. Lake joined the staff at Apple Valley High School for Girls in 2007 as a young teacher just out of teacher's college. She was a member of the science department led by a passionate, aggressive middle aged lady called Mrs. Grisham who always seemed to get what she wanted for her department. To ensure collaboration within her department, several teachers were asked to coordinate activities of the various grade levels. These activities included conducting four to six weeks weekly planning sessions, preparing examination scripts and circulating to teachers for feedback, coordinating marking of examination scripts, among other things. Despite her attempt at collaboration, there was always tension and quarrels in the department among the teachers and sometimes with herself. The task to coordinate grade 8 fell to Ms. Lake in 2009.

Nearing the time for the six weeks test which symbolized the end of the December semester, Ms. Lake prepared the grade 8 test and submitted the script to her colleagues for viewing. When Ms. Falconer saw it, she became disturbed as her students had not covered several of the topics on the test. She went to Ms. Lake who directed her to the head of the department (HOD). When she went to Mrs. Grisham, she was told the test was already set and she needed to figure out what she was going to do to get her students ready for the examination within such a short time span. A visibly furious Ms. Falconer made a report to the vice principal (VP) and explained that her students would not be able to sit the examination as the topics were new and she had not been informed that they should have been included in the six-week teaching and learning units. The VP called a meeting with all grade 8 science teachers along with the HOD.

During the meeting, it was revealed that of the eight teachers who taught grade eight, three of them were not aware of a change in topics. Ms. Lake explained that they were all absent from the planning meeting, so that may be the reason why they were unaware of the changes. Ms. Falconer, along with the others, protested that they had not known anything about the planning meeting. Ms. Lake stated that she had sent the information regarding the meeting as well as change in topics via email and no one had responded. They denied seeing same. Ms. Lake indicated that it was customary for her colleagues to be unresponsive to emails and she was tired of it. The VP asked the HOD if she was aware of the teachers' absence from the planning meeting and she said no. She thought everything was going according to plan as Ms. Lake had not reported any of this to her prior to today.

QUESTIONS FOR DISCUSSION:

9.   What are the issues in this case?

10. What do you think is the main problem in this case?

11. Do you think the Head of Department is supervising her team effectively? Why?

12. If you were Mrs. Grisham (HOD), how would you handle this situation?

13. If you were the vice principal what would your course of action be?

14. How could the department have prevented this matter from being taken to the vice principal?

15. Is there anything in the Education Code of Regulations that could address the issues identified in the script?

16. Conduct a needs assessment to ascertain if there is need for any professional development training based on the issue(s) in the case.

AM #12:
Clash of Heads

Ms. Waite, a teacher of mathematics and Mrs. Marshall, teacher of business studies, live in the same community and work at the same institution, Holy Family High School. Mrs. Marshall joined the staff two years prior to Ms. Waite.

It was March, the busiest period in the lives of 5th form teachers as School Based Assessment (SBAs) were due and teachers and students were trying frantically to complete them in order to meet the deadlines. Mrs. Marshall discovered that her desk and some boxes with students' SBA projects have been infested with rats. She reported this to the plant manager who searched her area and discovered several small rats. One of the boxes that contained rats was removed and placed close to the staff room's entrance for the workmen to remove in their daily cleaning. Two days later, Mrs. Marshall heard that another teacher was complaining about rats at her desk. She went to investigate and suggested that both herself and the other affected persons should write a report directly to the principal. When she got to the other side of the staffroom, Mrs. Marshall was confronted by Ms. Waite.

Ms. Waite (*angrily*): I don't know why you decide to carry your rats and put them close to other people's desk. (*She hisses her teeth*)

Mrs. Marshall: I didn't take the rats from my yard and put them here.

Ms. Waite: Aren't you the owner of the box? (*Looks up at her accusingly*)

Mrs. Marshall: It has the students' SBAs which makes it the property of Holy Family High School.

The exchange escalated and they had to be quieted by another colleague as they were disturbing other teachers. Students were also passing and staring through the window of the staffroom.

Mrs. Marshall: Galang with you big forehead. (*She walks away*)

Ms. Waite: Big like you p#$$%.

Mrs. Marshall went to the vice principal (VP) to make a complaint. When she got there, the VP was having dialogue with another colleague and told Mrs. Marshall to wait outside the door. Ms. Waite then showed up to make her own complaint. She was also asked to wait as the VP was currently with someone and another teacher was waiting. Ms. Waite looked Mrs. Marshall up and down, turned back to the VP and responded "Who is waiting? I don't see anybody". The VP realized that something was seriously wrong and ended her current meeting and invited both teachers inside her office. As they attempted to explain the situation, a shouting match ensued and Ms. Waite uttered "Can't bother with this @#$%^&" and stormed from the office. The VP explained to Mrs. Marshall that she was going to take the matter to the principal so she should write a report about what had happened. Mrs. Marshall begged the VP not to as she didn't want to get into any more trouble. The VP explained it was too late for that.

Both teachers were brought before the principal, Mr. Stokes, a fair but firm educator of many years. Mrs. Marshall explained that she thought they were both friends hence she felt comfortable making the comment but Ms. Waite exclaimed, "Friends? I don't like you. Me never like you yet. So get that out you head." This resulted in a shouting match during which a seemingly hurt Mrs. Marshall broke down in tears.

Both were given a strong reprimand by the principal and a memo about professional conduct which was placed on their files.

QUESTIONS FOR DISCUSSION:

26. What are the issues in this case?

27. How would you describe the actions of both teachers?

28. If you were any of the teachers in the case, what would you have done to prevent an escalation of the issue?

29. What would you do if you were the VP?

30. Do you think the course of action taken by the principal was appropriate? Is he too lenient or too harsh?

31. Is there anything in the Education Code of Regulation that addresses the issues identified in the cases?

32. Based on the issues, what professional development initiative is needed for the staff?

AM #13:
How Many Chances Are Too Many?

Marlon Grey was successful in his Grade Six Achievement Test and earned a coveted place at Greenwich High School. He started in September 2004. He was a very quiet and well behaved child who wore tested glasses with very thick lens. He was often teased by the other students about his glasses. One day he got frustrated and broke the glasses. His parents, though aware of this incident did not replace the tested glasses because they wanted to "punish" him.

As the seventh grade year progressed, Marlon's behaviour deteriorated. On November 21, 2004, his parents were called to school because of his constant disruptive behaviour in classes. February 19, 2005, while Marlon was being reprimanded for wearing the incorrect uniform to school, he verbally assaulted his form teacher Ms. Johnson. He was then suspended for five days. His parents were asked to return with him to school on the sixth day. During his absence, the principal asked Marlon's subject teachers to provide an academic and behavioural report about him. The reports indicated that his attendance and punctuality records were good but his grades were very low and he was defiant.

At the start of the September, 2005 school year, Marlon was made to repeat grade 7 as he was performing below standard. His attendance and punctuality records remained in good standing and there was improvement in some of his grades. However, he made very little friends with this new year group and was often seen in the company of students from his previous year group. On March 19, 2006, Marlon tried to borrow a book from another student, Jason, who refused to lend it to him. Marlon attacked Jason during the class. The teacher intervened but was met with strong resistance from Marlon who took his bag and left the class. He was once more suspended, this time for three days. His parents returned with him to school when the suspension ended. He was referred to the guidance counselor.

In September 2006, instead of matriculating to grade 8, Marlon was placed in grade 9. This was because the administration felt he was much bigger than the other boys in the year group and he would constantly beat upon them.

While in the ninth grade, on November 1, 2006, Marlon used a broken building block to break the arm of another student during an altercation. He was given the maximum suspension for causing grievous bodily harm to another student and his case was referred to the board. A letter was sent specifically to his father informing him of Marlon's behaviour and the school's action to refer the case to the board. After meeting, the board laid down some stipulations which included:

- Suspension is extended for another 5 days
- Must abide by all rules and regulations of the school
- Professional counselling and report submitted to school
- Peer counselling
- Academic improvement must be shown by December 2006
- Conduct and in particular respect to authority must improve

The principal asked teachers to submit weekly reports on Marlon. The reports revealed that whereas his attendance and punctuality records were good, grades were poor and he exuded extremely negative behaviour.

In January 20, 2007, Marlon disrupted biology class by verbally assaulting one of his classmates. When spoken to by his teacher, he told her several expletives and walked out of the class. He was suspended for another ten days for gross defiance. The principal requested another progress report which revealed that Marlon Grey:

- Does not respond to authority;
- is defiant;
- sits at back of class;
- does not do assignments;
- talks excessively in class; and
- is always poorly attired.

His case was again referred to the board who made the decision that he should be withdrawn from the school.

QUESTIONS FOR DISCUSSION:

21. Were there identified self-esteem issues that set the tone for a downturn in Marlon's behaviour?

22. Marlon made academic improvement when he repeated grade 7, yet his behaviour deteriorated. Why then was he allowed to jump to grade 9? What kind of strategy(ies) can be implemented to find a balance in this situation?

23. How do you believe jumping a grade level impacted Marlon?

24. How many chances are too many...when does a school say enough is enough?

25. How do you think a school can effectively monitor some of the recommendations made by the board?

26. Do you think decisions taken by the board on Marlon's second visit were an overkill?

27. Is there anything in the Education Code of Regulations/Child Care Protection Act that addresses the issue(s) identified in the case?

28. Can you identify any developmental initiative for staff and students based on the issues?

AM #14:
They Protested and Were Punished

Students at Great Joy High School for Girls were in high spirits as their annual sports day was fast approaching. One group of cheerleaders, the defending champions, decided to rehearse their routine in the national park during the short mid-term break. Their behaviour seemed to have been less than appropriate and caught the eyes and ears of the park security guard who placed a call to the school and reported the girls to the principal.

When school re-opened, the girls involved in the off-campus training were summoned to the office by Principal James. She gave the girls a strong reprimand and informed them that she was banning cheerleading competition from the annual sports day that year. She then made this announcement over the intercom and the excitement of all the girls turned to sadness. Despite the pleading of the student council body, the principal remained adamant.

The girls decided to register their protest and planned not to attend the sports day. The principal heard the rumours and the day prior to the event, made an announcement that every girl must be present at sports day. If they were not, only a written letter from their parents or a doctor's certificate would be accepted as an excuse. Otherwise, they would be severely punished. The girls were undaunted by this threat. Most of the school's population did not attend the sports day.

The Monday morning following the incident, Principal James instructed form teachers during the first registration period, to collect the letters from the students who were absent from the sports day. Those without a letter were withdrawn from classes and sent to the auditorium. It was 8:00 a.m.

While in the auditorium, they were made to stand in several lines on the stage adopting a strict military posture. This was done under the watchful gaze of the Prefects Body that was also pulled from classes to carry out this task. After an hour of doing this, the students were led outside to the school's playing field. They were now joined by Principal James. Again the students were made to adopt this military posture under the watchful eyes of the prefects while Principal James addressed them. This proved difficult for some students as the sun was hot, so several girls fidgeted. The girls who were caught fidgeting were sent to walk one lap around the 250m field in the sun. After Principal James addressed the students, she then proceeded to give them a series of physical activities to do. Some of the students started to cry. After the physical activities, the almost three hundred and twenty girls were instructed to walk in single file around the field three times. After the laps around the field, they had to stand still for thirty minutes on the netball court. When the time expired, Principal James addressed the girls once more and released them for classes. It was now 11:40 a.m.

QUESTIONS FOR DISCUSSION:

26. What are the main issues in this case?

27. Do you think the girls should have been punished since the initial incident did not happen on the school's compound?

28. How would you classify Principal James' decision to ban the cheerleading competition?

29. Was the series of punishment given to the girls too harsh?

30. How would you advise Principal James if you were an education officer and this was brought to your attention?

31. Who are some possible persons that could get involved in this situation?

32. Is there anything in the Education Code of Regulations or the Child Care Protection Act that speaks to the issues present in this case?

33. What professional development initiative can you identify based on the issue(s) in this case?

AM #15:
Vending at the School Gate

Russell Park Primary School has a population of over five hundred students. During lunch periods, some of the students would purchase their lunches from the vendors at the school gate because the lines at the school's tuck shop were too long, and also because they preferred the food sold by the vendors.

On Tuesday, February 10, 2013, several students purchased sprat fish and bread wrapped in a greasy brown paper bag from a vendor at the school gate. Later that day, several students fell ill and experienced vomiting and diarrhoea. Parents were called to take the children to the doctor. When they gathered on the school's compound, they became upset and demanded to speak with the principal as they felt that the school had been negligent and should be held responsible for what had happened to their children.

The principal pleaded with the parents to take the children to the doctor as that was the priority now. She promised to carry out a thorough investigation and share the findings with them.

As promised, an investigation was done and the principal discovered that the students who had fallen ill were the ones who had made their purchases at the school gate. The principal decided to meet with the vendors. It must be noted that this was not the first time that the principal had to speak to the vendors about vending at the gate and the types and state of foods that are sold to students.

It was also later discovered that the fish sold to the students were left over fish from the previous day.

QUESTIONS FOR DISCUSSION:

22. What are the main issues in the case?

23. Do you think the school should be held responsible for the illness of the students? Explain.

24. What strategies could be put in place by both parents and the school's administrators to prevent a recurrence of the incident?

25. Do you think sanctions should be levied against the vendor(s) for this action? If yes, please state course of action.

26. Is there anything in the Education Code of Regulations or the Child Care and Protection Act that addresses the issues identified in the case?

AM#16:
A Clash of Wills

Marcia Thorpe and Joanna Fairweather are both math teachers at Goodwill Academy. Ms. Thorpe has been working there for three years and Ms. Fairweather for four years. Both teachers had a good rapport with each other and often collaborated to successfully execute several projects. This was admired by the staff.

One day Ms. Fairweather approached Ms. Thorpe with an idea for a project to which Ms. Fairweather expressed uninterest without proferring a reason. This was the beginning of the nose dive of their relationship. As the term progressed, several seemingly minor incidents occurred between the two that led to a heightened sense of tension between them and the rest of the staff members who tried to intervene.

One day as Ms. Thorpe was standing on the corridor talking to a colleague, Ms. Fairweather passed by. In her passing, she seemed to have inadvertently bounced Ms. Thorpe, who stumbled a little. Ms. Fairweather did not apologize for this, neither did she stop. The colleague attempted to get her attention without much success.

Concern about the deterioration of their relationship circulated among the staff and eventually reached the ears of the principal. He met with both teachers separately about the matter.

A few months later, Ms. Thorpe stood in the staff lounge conversing with some colleagues when Ms. Fairweather entered and shoved Ms. Thorpe who toppled and fell in a chair that was nearby.

Ms. Thorpe: Wha' dat fa? (*Struggling to get up from the chair*)

Ms. Fairweather: What, you have a problem wid it? Come defen' it den.

Colleague: Guys, please stop...Ms. Fairweather, there was no reason for that.

Ms. Thorpe: But I don't know what this is about.

Ms. Fairweather: Well me say yuh fi defen' it if yuh have a problem.

(Ms. Thorpe gets up from the chair with much agility, bears down on Ms. Fairweather and delivers several blows to her face.)

A male colleague who seemed to have been the cause of the tension between the two "friends" intervened and stopped the fracas. When the principal heard about the matter, he referred the case to the board. After hearing the case, the board dismissed both teachers immediately. The teachers took the matter to the Jamaica Teacher's Association (the oversight body for teachers) who attempted to resolve the matter with the school. The principal was however, very resolute that he would not reinstate them. The matter was then taken to the court of arbitration. Six months after the incident, the court ruled that the teachers should be reinstated with immediate effect. The school year ended and they were not reinstated as the principal was adamant that the teachers would not be readmitted to the institution as they had allowed unprofessionalism to intrude on the school's relations.

Towards the beginning of the new school year, the concerned teachers, who by this time had resolved their issues and rebuilt their relationship, sought the intervention of the Ministry of Education (MoE). The MoE instructed the principal to reinstate the teachers with immediate effect. He did not comply with this. A second correspondence was sent requesting same and this was again ignored by the principal. A third correspondence was sent to the principal, but this time with a clause indicating that if he did not comply with the MoE instructions, then actions would be taken against him. By this time, it was the third week of the new school year. The institution then contacted both teachers and asked them to report to work immediately. The education officer met with both teachers before they returned and asked if they would be willing to accept a transfer. Ms. Fairweather was furious and adamant that she would not leave as she loved the school and was always comfortable. Ms. Thorpe indicated she would be willing to leave as long as her years of service and leave entitlement were not affected.

When both teachers returned to work, they were not issued with any timetable or resources. Instead they both sat in the staffroom all day. Ms. Fairweather went to the principal to ask about timetables and was dismissed. By the end of the day, a correspondence was sent from the MoE to release Ms. Thorpe to Johnson Bay School for Boys which was located ten miles from Goodwill Academy. The principal complied immediately. He then cautioned Ms. Fairweather about her rumoured relationship with the male member of staff and told her that any such repeat of display of jealousy and unprofessional behaviour would see her case again being referred to the board and next time, he would not relent.

QUESTIONS FOR DISCUSSION:

31. Identify the issues in the case.
32. Do you think the board's decision to dismiss the teachers with immediate effect was an appropriate one? Explain.
33. If you were the principal, what would your discussion be about when you first met with the teachers one-on-one?
34. If you were Ms. Thorpe, what would you have done to prevent the situation from escalating?
35. Discuss the JTA's action of taking the matter to the court. Is this the appropriate thing to have been done?
36. Examine the principal's defiant stance. Is it founded?
37. How do you think the actions of both teachers affected the morale of the staff?
38. Based on the issue(s), what professional development initiative can you identify?

39. Is there anything in the Education Code of Regulations that addresses the issue(s) identified in the case?

AM#17:
The Dismissal

Joy Maxwell is a science teacher at Goodwill High School. She is in the sixth month of her employment. Already, she has increased the number of students in the science club through her creativity. Despite being able to motivate her students, Ms. Maxwell seems not to get along well with the members of her department.

One day Ms. Maxwell had a conflict with a senior member of her department which resulted in an open confrontation inside the staffroom in the presence of other teachers. The matter was taken to the school's administrator who issued Ms. Maxwell with a memo for insubordination. She was also told by the principal that further dialogue would be had about the situation.

Three weeks later, the principal informed Ms. Maxwell that the institution would have to terminate her employment. However, Ms. Maxwell was offered three months' salary in advance, if she decided to resign voluntarily, and to prevent a letter of termination from being placed on her file.

QUESTIONS FOR DISCUSSION

1. What are the main issues in the case?
2. Do you think the situation was appropriately handled by the administration?

3. What could the institution have done to improve relations with Ms. Maxwell and the members of the department?

4. Do you think the institution was justified in dismissing Ms. Maxwell in the manner they did?

5. If you were Ms. Maxwell what would you have done?

6. Based on the issues, what professional development initiative can you identify?

7. Is there anything in the Education Code of Regulations that addresses the issues identified in the case?

AM#18:
She Knocked the Wind Out of Their Sails

Ms. Black was in her fifth year of employment at Bend Down High School.

In her third year, she received a letter from the school's administration informing her that her probation had been extended for another year. She received another such letter in her fourth year.

In this her fifth year, 2012, Ms. Black is unsettled because she has no intention of accepting another such letter. When she received the letter, it informed her that she had been appointed to the staff effective 2009.

Fast forward to 2014, two years later.

Ms. Black's classroom has several students making excessive noise that is disrupting the entire grades 9 & 10 block. Ms. Black isn't present. This had been happening for the past four years but has got more chronic in the last two years. Frequent absences and lateness. The teacher who taught next to Ms.

Black's classroom was at his wits end and for the fourth time, lodged a complaint to the principal and vice principals, this time in writing.

The vice principal started an investigation. The staff attendance register revealed that Ms. Black had been absent on the days she reported to have been present, and late on days she reported to have been early. The VP also observed and gathered other evidence of Ms. Black's frequent absence from her classes. The parents of several students wrote letters to the institution about Ms. Black's delinquency and expressed concerns about the numerous classes their children were missing.

The VP reported the matter to the principal; Ms. Black was called in. She attempted several excuses but then realized she had to tell the truth because the evidence was against her. Ms. Black was brought before the school board, where she confessed and admitted to being guilty of the things brought against her. She pleaded with the board for mercy after explaining her situation and it was granted.

Ms. Black started demonstrating improvement in her attitude towards work. Three months later, she went back to the old ways.

Ms. Black, despite her frequent absences, whenever she was present, she would spend the time preparing students for the national speech and drama festival. The students would sometimes do well, earning several gold and silver medals.

One day the principal called a staff meeting. When the teachers went, to their surprise, the principal unveiled a new initiative she had developed called the principal's award. For this, teachers were awarded in three categories. A letter of commendation given on regular white letter size paper to teachers who were performing satisfactorily but not at the highest level; The Blue Ribbon Award, which was a letter of commendation given with a blue ribbon décor to teachers who were performing above a satisfactory level; and the third and highest award, The Gold Ribbon Award, which was a letter of commendation given with a gold ribbon décor to a teacher who demonstrated well-rounded and outstanding performance. The teachers thought it was a great idea but as the awards were being presented, the excitement turned to anger and resentment. A hushed silence fell over the room as several teachers who were viewed as the backbone of the institution by colleagues, students and administrative staff were awarded blue ribbons, while Ms. Black was awarded the principal's Gold Ribbon Award (and was not on hand to receive it as she was absent). By the end of the presentation there was a palpable tension in the room. The principal awkwardly said thank you and dismissed the meeting.

Some persons attempted to request a meeting with the principal to discuss the situation but this was denied by the principal initially. This refusal only heightened the tension between the principal and the staff members. Several projects and initiatives were now in jeopardy because the individuals who were considered the backbone of the institution, and received the Blue Ribbon Award, were giving up on the projects and initiatives they had started. One senior teacher intervened and persuaded the principal to meet with the staff to solve the situation.

At the meeting the teachers inquired of the principal the criteria that were used to determine awards but she could not provide a definitive response. Instead she revealed she used the files of teachers and what she saw on a daily basis. She further indicated she did not form a committee but did it by herself because she wanted it to have her personal touch.

QUESTIONS FOR DISCUSSION

1. What are the issues you identify in this case?

2. How do you view the series of letters received by Ms. Black over the five-year period? Why do you believe the letters were issued?

3. Are there any legal implications for those actions (the letters)?

4. Do you think the classroom teacher who reported Ms. Black through writing did the right thing? Why?

5. How do you think the complaint from the teacher done in writing impacted the decision of the vice principal to do the investigation?

6. Is there any conclusion you can draw about the administration management of the institution? If so what are those conclusions?

7. Do you think Ms. Black should have been given a Gold Ribbon Award? Why?

8. How do you think the principal could have prevented the idea of the awards from disrupting staff morale?

9. Is there anything in the Education Code of Regulations that addresses the issues identified in the case?

10. Can you identify any professional developmental initiative for staff and administrators? What would it be?

PART 2:

Testimonials

The Toolkit of Testimonial Compartment

From the Horse's Mouth

A well-known Jamaican proverb says "if fish come from water bottom and say it is deep, believe him". Why is that, you ask. If I were the fish I would respond "I live it everyday". So, what more credibility would you need? What does this have to do with this text? Each place of learning is different and has its own demands. The challenges faced by educators daily are vast and extremely diverse, hence quick thinking and creativity is constantly needed. Often, some of these creative and effective approaches go unnoticed. No theoretical studies can replace the experience of a teacher-tried and proven. In organizations, testimonials aid in the building of the brand; gives credibility. Therefore, this section provides a toolkit of testimonials from teachers and administrators who have been working indefatigably in the Jamaican education system for a number of years. The testimonies explain challenges that these educators have faced and the strategies they employed to overcome the challenges. I hope you will find it useful.

It All Happened in Ten Minutes

Keisha Foster-McFarlane has been a teacher for over eleven years. She teaches biology to grades 10, 11 and 6th form (some cultures refer to it as grades 12 & 13).

It is the time of year when School Based Assessment projects (SBAs) are due to be submitted and the Caribbean Secondary Education Studies examination right on its heels. There have been several complaints from teachers about the grade 11 students going off to work on their SBAs instead of attending classes. This is creating a hindrance in them completing the syllabus in time for examination. Being cognizant of the repercussions of such action, I decided to give my form class (grade 11-2) a pep talk as to why this action of missing classes to complete SBAs is not a prudent decision.

While speaking to them, one bold student interjected.

Student 1: I pay my money for my exam already and I can't afford to fail so I need to complete my SBAs.

Me: If you complete the SBAs and do not go to the class, then you may still fail as the syllabus would not have been completed and so you would not be able to answer the questions on the exam paper.

Student 1: Well Miss, I made that choice and when I did, I didn't know my other classmates would have made a similar decision.

Me: But you had all of the December holiday to do the SBAs.

Student 1: Miss not all of us have computers at home. Plus, I have to print and I do not have that facility at home so it didn't make any sense. I cannot print here on campus because it is too expensive. The cyber-centre rates are better. Those close by a certain time in the afternoon so I have to wait until they are open at 9:30 in the mornings to go there. That means I must miss classes.

Student 2:   But Miss, why can't the school organize itself in such a way that the SBAs can be done earlier in the school year so we don't have to be pressured so close to exams?

Student 3:   Well nobody can control what I do. My SBAs must be completed. My mother doesn't have a problem with my going to the cyber centre at that time so that's final. It is the school that must get in order. (*She crossed her arms and pouted. The entire class started talking at once.*)

I indicated for them to be quiet. When they did, I launched into what I thought was a brilliant speech about the importance of coming to school, attending classes, being punctual and the list goes on. They were very quiet as I spoke and I thought they were all hanging on to every word. At the end of my speech, student 3 stood up and started clapping slowly and tentatively, with every sound from her hands dripping with sarcasm. She was then joined by student 2, and six others, followed by the rest of the class. I felt the bile rise to my throat and my cheeks felt flushed with anger. I attempted to speak but was at a loss for words. Worst yet because of my stutter, whenever I get angry, words and fluent speech eludes me. So as not to make myself a spectacle, all I could utter were the words "Good afternoon ladies" and walked from the classroom. The girls looked around in amazement as they thought I was about to punish them.

The following morning I went back to the form room to conduct registration; the girls were very quiet and the atmosphere pensive. I conducted the devotional exercise and I did not mention the prior afternoon's incident. For the entire week I kept going to the form room both mornings and afternoons and I still did not address it. All this time, I was thinking about what I could do to these girls that would be a punishment but instructive at the same time. Punishment should not embarrass but teach lessons and encourage transformation, and this was what I wanted for the girls in my form.

On Monday of the following week, I went to take the afternoon register. After prayers, I told the girls to spare me ten minutes (10 mins) of their time as I would like to share a life lesson with them. Some persons complained that they had a bus to catch or their parents were waiting. Some wanted to leave but my facial expression, one of *'you better not push it…or else'* somehow made them comply. I launched into a pep talk about the qualities that they currently have, qualities that they lack, what the world wants and what they do not have…how to achieve success…negative traits that prevent personal positive growth. This action I did every day for an entire month. Oh yes! Every. Day. This meant they were always ten minutes late for any after-school activity. They did not like it especially on evenings when they had cheerleading, dance rehearsals or any activity that they loved. Then students eventually started anticipating what the next pep talk would be about. It was interesting that during one of the pep talks, one student got up and chided the young ladies who instigated the sarcastic cheer to my original pep talk about their attendance to class.

I ended the daily ten-minute session when one morning during the registration process, the student who instigated the cheer said to me "Miss, thank you for the talks in the afternoons I really enjoy them. They have been really good and I have learnt a lot. I am sorry about the cheer. I just wanted to have the last say and see you hurt because sometimes I feel you think you are always right." That acknowledgement and apology initiated a silence that was weighted with anticipation. I accepted it and told them thanks. That same afternoon, when they sat down and expected the pep talk, I apologized to them for not recognizing how they were feeling and then I sent them home. First they were hesitant as they were not sure if I was serious. When they realized I was serious, they all laughed. Some left immediately while others loitered around requesting that I talk to them about a life lesson. I looked back and thought yes, I had achieved my objective of administering punishment while teaching valuable lessons. Seeing the value in discussing these life lessons, I still did it with them but only for two days a week until the school year ended.

The students were not the only ones who benefited. These ten-minute sessions led to open, honest expressions that caused me to reflect on my approach and communication style. I was unaware the students had the perception that I believed I was 'always right'.

Our communication improved. The students and I expressed more mutual respect for each other: I respected their unique personal talents and gifts; they respected and appreciated that I was able to see their low level of maturity and recognizing it for what it truly was, and choosing to do something else besides purely punishing them. The punishment only option would have ended up in resentment and possibly a tug for classroom power. The *strong, vocal student bullies* vs. *teacher* is a recipe for continued insolence and ensuing disaster, while what I really want is for all to be on the same side with the same goal. The goal of being successful in their examinations.

FOOD FOR THOUGHT:

a. Explore the benefits of punishment that is designed for rehabilitation.
b. Reflect on the negative consequences that can result from punishment that is purely punitive.

Classroom Crack-Up

Antonio Bartley has been a teacher of physics for over 10 years.

While I will beat my chest and tout myself as a great teacher, I will not imply it was always this way. Teaching in an all girls institution is no easy feat. At the beginning, I experienced moments where I was challenged in class by girls and this made class control and managing behaviour difficult. I even wondered if this was for me. I started trying different strategies in an attempt to get a handle on things. This led to my discovery of the comedian in me. Oh yes! That is exactly what I said. Comedian. I realized that whenever a situation arises, I am able to diffuse it with my wry humour.

One day two students began arguing openly on the corridor and then moved into the classroom:

Girl 1:   You are rude. Do not talk to me like that.

Girl 2:   Watch here, is who you?

Girl 1:   What did you just say to me?

Girl 2:   Did I just stutter?

Immediately I said to both students non-threateningly:

Me: Just beat a gyal mek me see, but the winner must be prepared to fight me (*howling like a martial artiste and getting into my version of crouching tiger stance*).

The entire class started laughing including the girls who were arguing. That diffused the situation and I was able to commence my class smoothly.

In another instance, we were trying to work through a formula but the girls were quite restless and were not cooperating. I paused to enquire about any challenges they were having and they complained about being tired and not in the mood. I asked them to state the consequences if they were to approach all subjects in this way. "Sir I am not thinking about that now. I just can't wait to leave school and get a job", one bold student explained.

"What kind of job do you intend to get without qualification, especially if you do not complete high school successfully?" I replied in a soft tone.

"Well sir, I'm sure work must easier than this!" she exclaimed and some students chuckled.

"Well the easiest job to find is in the field of prostitution and you neither have the body nor the temperament for that. Besides, such a pretty face and a brilliant mind must make you CEO of a worthwhile enterprise; not the streets," I responded mockingly. The girls laughed and we chatted for another minute and then it was back to the lesson. I was able to proceed without further difficulty.

I always try to find humour in the negative and steer it to the positive. I didn't accomplish this overnight. It came with building a relationship with the girls. I try to understand their world; give them leverage to express themselves once it is done respectfully; share my experiences with them; greet them at the classroom door; engage them in small talk before classes and during the two-minute breaks I sometimes give, address issues one-on-one. Most importantly is that I set boundaries and ensure that I maintain those boundaries. This way, I was able to build healthy relationships that allowed for my use of humour without it affecting standards of the classroom or breach school policies.

It is the consistent application of these strategies that have propelled me to this place of comfort in the classroom after ten years. This strategy may not work for everyone, and at all times, but it sure has worked and is still working for me.

FOOD FOR THOUGHT:

a.   Discuss the value of humour in the classroom.
b.   What are some other strategies that can be used to reach students at their level?

When Being at Odds Stacked the Odds Against Them

Rayon Simpson is a stalwart educator with over ten years' experience at varying levels of the education sector, including being a principal.

Two members of staff could not get along. This was a situation I inherited when I was promoted to principal of Belvedere Academy. This poor relationship between the two often negatively impacted the activities and morale of the entire staff. One day after one of their rivalries was on display, I summoned both of them to my office. They came in with much trepidation, almost certainly expecting a meeting of a mediatory fashion and reprimand. I said absolutely nothing about the matter. Instead, I informed them that there was a reading programme that the Ministry of Education (MoE) through our region was spearheading and I needed both of them to work on a programme for our school to fit the profile and expectations of the MoE. They were silent for about five minutes then they asked why them. "I just believe both of you want to do much better at interrelations and thought this opportunity would give you that chance," I responded. They accepted, but what followed wasn't anything close to docile acceptance. Soon thereafter, they were emailing me to ask for one-on-one meetings. Almost every time it was to discuss the cruelty of my placing them to work as a team, the fact that they were not seeing eye to eye, and whether or not I could discontinue the arrangement. Each time, I listened, and then at the end asked the complainer if I could invite the other team member to join the meeting now. The answer was always no. The message clearly sunk in that I was not interested in small talks about anyone. Each week I would require updates from both of them, thus they were forced to collaborate. Pretty soon they started to discover things about each other that they admired.

I was vigilant enough to record each session I had with them during the intervention process. While I did not articulate it, they knew me well enough to have known that it meant if they did not work out their issues, I would have had enough information to prove that I had intervened. Thus, I would have solid grounds on which to make whatever recommendations I thought fit to the school board. Notwithstanding, the meetings were always respectful and devoid of intimidations.

During the life of the project, I learned that they were very good teachers with very high expectations but with different methods and mindsets which was perfectly normal. I also surmised that they were committed teachers and would go the extra mile to get work done and to be recognized by their colleagues. The main problem was that they saw each other as threats. The knowledge garnered from this situation helped me to develop a staff incentive programme whereby staff members contributed a specified amount from their salary each month; this was placed in a revolving fund and one member of staff (faculty and non-teaching) had an opportunity of winning a scholarship valued at one hundred thousand dollars ($100,000.00) each academic year. Consider this: the basic idea for this scholarship came from the two ladies who were at odds and the general school populace refined it.

There was also a "Staff of the Term Programme" whereby winners were selected based on attendance, lesson plan submission, participation in extra-curricular activities, etc. There was a rubric used to measure each indicator so it was very objective and transparent. The winner got a plaque, five thousand dollars ($5,000.00) and their photo publicly displayed. Both teachers have won it since my intervention.

I must confess that they are still not bosom buddies and they still silently carry grudges for each other. But they do not publicize it because they are not sure what I will do next.

FOOD FOR THOUGHT:

Discuss the impact that staff incentive/welfare programmes can have on staff morale and team building.

Time Out in Three Minutes

Dennis Jackson has been an educator for over ten years with extensive experience in multi-cultural instructions and differentiated classrooms.

(name changed)*

I can recall my anxieties as a young, new teacher in the secondary school system. For the first couple of months, I thought daily about what the principal asked me in the job interview: "Tell me something, you don't look a day older than some of our boys, how do you plan to manage their behaviour and make them respect you?" He seemed to have bought the response I whipped up, but I wondered daily if in reality I could command the attention and respect of the students. It didn't take me long to admit that a particular grade 10 class was intent on giving me an ulcer. I spoke to their homeroom teacher about the challenge I was having with them and she expressed that she shared my sentiments. I was thankful that I only saw them once per week for drama, but truly wished it was a double period before lunch so I wouldn't have to deal with their sugar intake. Their sugar high from lunch did not help with their natural hyperactive tendencies. It was the only class I felt I had to work especially hard to get settled to take the register and proceed with my starter activity.

One day out of frustration, I spontaneously came up with a strategy that worked wonders in shaping the behavioural patterns of the students. I must admit that my intention was to punish the students but what was born was a tool that helped us all in more ways than one. The strategy is my version of *Time Out*.

With a timer in hand, perfectly visible to all the students, I announced that *Time Out* will begin (counting down audibly) in 5, 4, 3, 2, 1. That was usually just to get their attention. It works well especially if they are used to the strategy.

Before truly beginning their *Time Out*, I remind them of the rules:

"For approximately **60 seconds***, every one is expected to remain perfectly still and perfectly quiet. Since I am a nice and reasonable teacher I will allow* **three opportunities** *for this* **60 second** *period to be broken. If you choose to break this period's perfect stillness and perfect silence* **three times***, then you will have to sit in Time Out for* **2 minutes***. Again because I am a nice and reasonable teacher I will allow* **two opportunities** *for this* **2-minute** *period to be broken. If you choose to break this period's perfect stillness and perfect silence* **two times***, then you will have to sit in Time Out for* **3 minutes***.*

Again because I am a nice and reasonable teacher I will allow **one opportunity** *for this* **3-minute** *period to be broken. If you choose to break this period's perfect stillness and perfect silence, then you will have to sit in Time Out for the remainder of the entire session…in perfect still and perfect silence."*

With a timer in hand, perfectly visible to all the students, I then proceed to say: *"60 seconds of absolute stillness and silence will begin now."*

In my ten years of practice, using this strategy with different age groups, I can only recall three times that I have actually gone up to three minutes of *Time*

Out and one occurrence when the three-minute period was broken. And of course the students had to sit quietly for the entire double period. I find it works best if I am unrelenting. I don't give chances. So for the cynic who is going to cough or purposely clear his or her throat, the timer will get reset. Hence, *"2 minutes of absolute stillness and silence will begin now!"* **However, it is important that a pleasant tone is used when the rules are being given or when you are announcing the start of a new time period**. It prevents the students from being confrontational. What I have noticed too is if a child legitimately has to scratch or make themselves comfortable on a chair or cough, they tend to raise their hand. **I never ignore such a student**. I go to them and allow them to whisper to me, whatever they need to do, and permit the adjustment while keeping an eye on the others.

The response of the grade 10 students I mentioned is why I haven't abandoned the practice. I can recall a female student after the first improvised instance with the strategy blurting out "Sir is the first I've ever heard us quiet!" The others as a chorus agreed. One boy shouted out "Sir mek we dweet again." The consensus made it hard to say no. The class ran smoothly afterwards. The following week they returned with the same restless energy and I immediately held up my timer. By the way, if you are going to use your watch, perhaps you should intentionally make them see you remove it from your wrist. If it's a stopwatch or small clock, make them see you going for it. It communicates that you are merely responding to a behaviour choice they have made.

Anyway, it worked well the second week and the class ran smoothly. The following week I was surprised that they settled on their own relatively well so I proceeded to take the register only to hear "Sir so what happen to *Time Out*?" I responded suggesting that they didn't need it today. In their minds it wasn't the punishment I expected it to be, but instead it became a starter game. I submitted to their request and repeated it. I started several of their classes in this manner although it was clear to them that the strategy was no longer needed. I should mention that I was approached by their homeroom teacher who wanted to know about *Time Out* and what I had been doing with them. Repeatedly she noticed that whenever she had a difficultly settling the students someone would yell "*Time Out*". She eventually inquired of the class monitor what the others were referring to, who told her to come and talk to me about it. At the end of the term she came again and commented on the marked improvement of the students' conduct and reported that she started seeing improvements in their grades as well. In fact, at the end of the year, ten of the students made it to the principal's honour roll. The following year some of the same students, including those who were not on the honour roll, achieved an average that warranted them graduating with honours. This teacher served as the students' homeroom teacher for two years prior to them entering my classroom, and had started agreeing with several colleagues that these students were the hopeless among the cohort.

It makes me want to take a *Time Out* to think.

FOOD FOR THOUGHT:

Is there space for innovation and creativity in managing student behaviour?

Right Under Our Noses

**Lisa Haughton is an educator with over ten years of experience in the classroom and performing administrative work.*
(name changed)*

When I joined the staff at *Happy Valley High School, the empty chairs and lethargic attitude at staff development sessions did not escape my notice. It didn't take me long to surmise that the several empty chairs was a regular occurrence. In the back of my mind, I started wondering what could be the cause of this state of apathy. I continued doing my duty as a teacher and as I started becoming more involved in other aspects of education, my competence as an educator grew rapidly. This was further confirmation that continued professional development of educators was mandatory. One day I instinctively started talking to random teachers about their level of involvement or lack thereof in school activities, especially the staff development seminars. I discovered from these conversations that what was missing was broad-based planning and participation. Teachers felt left out of the planning of their own development. As I contemplated these things, I carefully observed the staff and attempted to garner information on their various competences. To my surprise, Happy Valley High School was equipped with a highly qualified and competent staff in other areas besides their subject area of specialization. I began to understand why the teachers felt left out and underutilized.

While pursuing my Master's Degree in Education Leadership, the idea of a Professional Development Unit (PDU) came to me. This unit would be responsible for the planning and execution of staff development seminars with some of the presenters being members of staff. This would get teachers more involved in their own development. I sought audience with my vice principal and proposed the idea to her. She loved it. This idea was thrown out to the staff at one of our staff meetings and they loved it immediately. The first step was to have the staff volunteer to be members of the team. This was the first step towards an inclusive /collaborative effort. Since then, teachers' involvement in the staff development seminars have improved. The frequently empty chairs have decreased and so have the lethargic attitudes.

I saw the need for something more to be done for the staff and even though I was only a classroom teacher, I didn't allow that to be a deterrent. I took the idea to administration; they listened and decided to try. Had my vice principal shunned my idea, I would not know the potential impact of such an idea. Through this, I have discovered my growing competence as a budding administrator. The initiative revealed that school administrators must listen to their staff, assess ideas, and implement where possible. It is all about a collaborative approach. Most importantly, sometimes we are looking outside to find the 'right' people to conduct seminars for educators when the 'right' people are right in front of us. So, if you are experiencing a similar challenge within your institution, maybe a PDU is what you need to create transformation.

FOOD FOR THOUGHT:

Consider the potential impact on education if teachers were to be empowered to contribute to its development in a sustained and structured way.

The Day I Became a Part of Their World

Dorraine Reid has been an educator for over ten years and has had the privilege to serve in different areas of the sector.

I entered the classroom and was greeted with the words "yes goody reach" followed by a haughty laugh that drowned out my cheerful good morning, which indicated that the room was filled with young people. Teenagers to be exact. I looked around suspiciously and inquired if all was well, and the same voices teasingly responded in unison, "Yes goody". In my ignorance I asked what the term meant and they all laughed again. One student explained "Miss it is just a term we use". As the class proceeded I realized that the term "goody" was being thrown around the class as they referred to each other. So I asked them if they all called each other "goody", how would they know who is being referred to at a particular time. Again they laughed and looked at me as if I was from a different planet, then explained that they understood each other because they have been doing it for some time. In the same breath, they expressed that I needed to get with it. Can you imagine how stunned I was? Stunned but not upset. I was actually happy they were comfortable to share their world with me.

In this class there was a student called *Rochelle. Sometimes I have grave difficulty getting her to do any work. This particular day, Rochelle sat sucking her thumb and wasn't participating. As class progressed, I asked her quite nicely to be my scribe for the day by making jottings on the board inside the classroom. At first she was very hesitant. Then suddenly I said, "Come on goody bops, today you are in charge." The moment the words were out of my mouth, the room erupted with laughter, including Rochelle. She said, "Miss you learn it fas' man." I responded with my most award winning smile. She got up, took up the whiteboard marker and got to work. I made sure to address her using the term "goody" for the remainder of the class. She loved it, became animated and remained that way throughout the rest of the class. The other students enjoyed my immersion into their world and took pleasure in correcting me whenever I used the term inappropriately.

Two days later, as I was walking across the school compound, I was accosted by a group of five girls from that same class. They expressed how long they had been trying to find me. In my most facetious tone I asked why they were hunting me as if I were lost. Being used to me by now they didn't even acknowledge it but pressed on with their mission. They explained that some of them were in trouble because of a picture of a classmate they had circulated on social media. I listened as they told their story of how it came to be. One bold student said "Miss we are going to tell you everything, even the bad part and all we are asking is that you explain to Ms. Jones (the school's vice principal) because she is not listening to us. But Miss she can't know all of the bad part. It's confidential. We only telling you cause we can talk to you and we want you to understand the full story." So I looked at them and provokingly asked why they think I need to hear their secret. Again they ignored me and continued talking. At the end of the story, I gave them my opinion in a rather frank way and they took it graciously. They even looked contrite and apologized when I admonished some of their actions.

You may ask what is the significance of this. I was able to reach one student and engage the rest of the class by being open to their world. Had I taken a different approach and told them not to use such words in my class, the atmosphere in the class would have been different. What those students saw was a teacher who appreciated their world and tried to understand it. This world is very important to them and whenever they attempt to let you in, it is an opportunity you should take while maintaining your position as their teacher. If you are shut out of this world, you will never be able to reach them.

Students live in the information age where they are bombarded with data and sometimes do not know what to do with it. That is why when they came to me with a social media situation, I accommodated them because they needed a sounding board. They needed someone to bring clarity to the situation instead of punishment. Who best to do that for them than the teacher who understands their world? Teaching that class became more enjoyable.

FOOD FOR THOUGHT:

Examine the importance of meeting students at their level and how this can build a relationship based on trust and mutual understanding.

I Tried But Didn't Read
Between the Lines

Barbara Johnson has been an educator for over 15 years and an administrator for 10 years.

(name changed)*

When I became vice principal (VP) of Toll Park High School I was very excited. I had a love for administrative work and this was the perfect opportunity for me to enhance my competences. Toll Park High School was a shift system institution situated in one of the inner cities in Kingston; hence, most of its populace were students from nearby garrisons. I tried to be a hands on VP who stamped her authority from very early in the 'game'. I refused to be partial and I was not afraid to stand my ground. Because of the school's location, it was often invaded by supposedly bad men from the surrounding communities, who would often prey on students and teachers. Whenever this happened, I was not afraid to confront them and tell them to leave, neither was I hesitant to call the police despite the numerous threats I received. I soon came to be known as the no-nonsense and fearless VP.

I made my presence felt among students, teachers and ancillary staff. I observed them carefully. That was how I met the grade 10 student on the first shift that caused me grave concern. I will call him Mark. The first time I saw his eyes, my body became clothed in goose pimples. They were a deep, dark, black hole. Chilling to the bone. He spoke very little and never smiled. He had a very stony expression.

I observed that the students and some teachers alike were very fearful of him. An investigation into his background revealed that Mark was from a single parent home; his mother worked minimum wage, and he had a younger sibling. All three of them lived in a two-bedroom structure in the inner city community known as South West. The most chilling but not shocking information was that he was a member of a community gang that was known for slinging guns and carrying out numerous criminal activities. As I absorbed the details of the information, I realized there and then that I had to tread carefully with this one. When I checked his grades, I realized he was doing fairly well. After giving much thought to his situation, I thought to myself, "I will have to make a friend out of this one." How? I wasn't sure but I knew I would find a way.

I made it my duty to walk the grade 10 block a little more frequently than the others. I would stop by Mark's classroom and observe the class. I would sometimes walk around the classroom and look in the students' books, including Mark's. I commended their writing skills, neatness of work, and completion of assignments. When I saw him on the compound, I would engage him in dialogue but I would involve the other students so that my intention towards Mark would not be obvious. One day, I asked the form teacher to give me grades for the students in the class. I called a few of them to my office one at a time. When Mark came, I expressed my ignorance about his ability and how pleased I was with his performance. I ignored his stony expression. I discussed with him ways he could improve in some areas. By the end of my thirty-minute talk with him, we both agreed that he would stop by my office to let me see his book and test papers regardless of the grades.

Through our frequent interactions, we developed a very good relationship. Towards the end of the grade 10 academic year, he confided that he may not return to school. I encouraged him not to be a dropout, and counselled him. I made a deal with him that if he returned to grade 11, I would assist him with back to school. When he told this to his mother, she was very happy and called me expressing her gratitude for taking such an interest in her son's well-being.

September morning, the beginning of the new school year, Mark returned to grade 11, and I remained true to my promise and assisted him. He eventually confided in me his status as a gang member and his desire to get out of it. I continued to counsel him, and his grades improved. Even his interaction with his classmates improved. One October morning as the school got ready for worship, news came that Mark was shot and killed. It was like I received a crippling punch in the gut that was slowly killing me. I cried.

Later in reflection, I realized that while I did all I could to save Mark, I made some errors. First was that I tried doing it alone without seeking help from organizations that could have assisted. This assistance would have helped me to eventually get him out of the community. Mark did not confide in me his desire to leave because he wanted me to know; he said it because he wanted me to help him get out. I recognized this too late.

The fact is, as administrators, we must find ways to help our students. Immerse yourselves in their lives. Listen to the things that they tell you but more so, listen to the unspoken words in the spoken words. No student is hopeless. You just need to find the strategy that works best for you.

FOOD FOR THOUGHT:

Is it reasonable to expect teachers to immerse themselves in the lives of all troubled students that cross their paths?

The Dismantling of Double Timetables

**Deloris James is an educator for over 15 years. She served as vice principal for five years and as a principal for five years.*
(name changed)*

I have been teaching at Grant Wood High School for a number of years. When the post of vice principal became vacant, I saw it as the perfect opportunity to utilize my administrative skills. I applied and was successful. Grant Wood High was a shift school and I was working on the first shift at the time of my permanent appointment. Hence, I had sole responsibility for the administrative affairs on that shift.

There were some teachers who were happy with my appointment. There were those who thought the job was supposed to be theirs and I was less than deserving of the post, hence, they refused to be compliant and supportive. As my first year as VP progressed, some teachers came around while there were others who didn't.

Even though I was responsible for the first shift, I occasionally had to interact with fellow colleagues on the second shift. During my brief interaction, I observed that there were some teachers who appeared to have had a great amount of free time. I was puzzled by it but couldn't do much as it was not my shift. The following year, the VP for the second shift who I will call Mrs. Black, was due for retirement and I was asked to take up the post of VP on the second shift. I accepted. My first task was to prepare a timetable for the new academic school year. Because I had no knowledge of this, I was asked to work closely with the outgoing VP in the timetable preparation. Mrs. Black informed me that we would schedule a time to meet during the holidays. However, the first week into the summer holiday, I received a call from Mrs. Black informing me that she went ahead and prepared the timetable and teachers have already received theirs. When I inquired why I wasn't contacted, she explained that since I would have quite a bit to do, she was trying to make my transition from the first shift to second shift easier. I expressed my gratitude.

Three weeks after that, while in full preparation mode for my role on this new shift, I looked at the timetables. I somehow felt uneasy about it. I decided to engage the expertise of a fellow colleague at a university. He came with a second person. As the three of us browsed the master timetable sheets we found some discrepancies and adjusted the timetables. I had the timetables for the teachers reprinted.

At the staff development seminar at the beginning of the new school year, I recalled all timetables and distributed the new ones. Upon examination of the timetables recalled, I found out that some teachers had two timetables. One timetable that was outfitted with the required amount of sessions per week and another that had less than half the required amount of sessions. Further investigation into the matter revealed that the timetable with the required sessions were used to present to the education officers when they visited the school, while the other was used for teaching purposes. As a result, some teachers had more than the required sessions.

The teachers who benefited from this were very angry with the new timetables. They complained miserably despite my explanation that the timetables had to be re-worked because it must be in keeping with what is stipulated in the Education Code of Regulations. When they realized I was unrelenting, they stopped complaining directly and decided to make my job more difficult. To register their protests, they conspired and dismissed an entire block of students thirty minutes before school was scheduled to be over. This disrupted the entire school as the students were boisterous and congregated at the school gate demanding to be let out as their teachers indicated school was finished for the day.

The following day I called all the teachers together who were responsible, gave them a strong reprimand and told them they would be given a memo that would be placed on their file. I informed them that if I had another protest in any form that negatively impacted teaching and learning activities, a letter would be sent to the ministry informing them of their professional misconduct, and they would be brought before the school board.

Still not satisfied, they secretly planned a protest by the school gate to have me removed. When I got word about the scheduled protest, I immediately contacted the board and requested that the main instigator be transferred to the first shift with immediate effect. This request was granted. With the main instigator no longer on the second shift, the scheduled protest fell through. Slowly and gradually, even though some of those teachers secretly held grudges, things proceeded normally.

The lesson in all of this is: do not be afraid to acknowledge your shortcomings and seek help. I am glad I sought the expertise of fellow colleagues. The sharing of best practices is very important to the successful running of an organization. Secondly, stand your ground even if you are standing alone. Be firm and decisive. Had I not done these things, I would not have been able to quell the uprise that was mounting against me.

FOOD FOR THOUGHT:

a. Discuss the challenges that can result from attempts to change the culture of an organization.
b. Examine the importance of school administrators understanding and using change management strategies.

Counting Down & Raising Hands in the Name Of Discipline

Diedre Dixon has been an educator for over fifteen years. During this time she has served in the capacity of grade supervisor and dean of discipline.

When I just started teaching, I had difficulty getting my students to settle down. One day, as they were proving to be more challenging than other times, I folded my arms and started counting down; one minute after school, two minutes after school, three minutes after school…I continued saying this until the students picked up what was happening. Eventually the noise in the class died. By then, I was at fifteen minutes. That afternoon, I kept them back for fifteen minutes and they had to sit quietly without speaking to each other. That afternoon I told them that the next time things got to fifteen minutes I would double it.

The lesson of this is to honour your promise even if it is for one minute. Be creative with that one minute. When my students earn the punishment to be held back for one minute, I ensure that they sit unmoving for the one minute with the condition that if there is any movement or sound, the one minute starts all over. This usually gets them quiet.

Sometimes I would use a hand raising strategy. This usually precedes the countdown. When the noise level increases and students are talking out of turn, I would raise my hand. The moment my hand goes up, the rest of the class should hold up their right hand without speaking. The only person allowed to speak at this point is me. I would walk around the class at this point and any student found non-compliant is asked to fall in line. When I have the full attention of all the students I would remind them of the rules, and continue my class. If they continue to talk then I use the countdown strategy.

Students do not like to stay back after school, especially if they have activities that they enjoy doing. Hence, I found this strategy to be effective. The impact of the strategy on the students was long lasting as during their graduation ceremony, it was one of the things they recalled.

FOOD FOR THOUGHT:

Discuss the impact that honouring promises in the classroom has on the students' behaviour.

Behaviour Probation

Suan Daley has been an educator for eight years. During that time, she served as a grade 8 supervisor.

The grade 8 cohort was a difficult group. On an average day, they would become involved in various confrontations and fights, which would often disrupt school activities. They were spoken to, held back after school and their parents contacted, yet their behaviour remained unchanged. I sat and thought long and hard about what to do as I knew the students could not continue this way. The idea of a behavioural probation form came to me. I met with fellow grade 8 teachers and proposed the idea to them and they all agreed. Together we sat down and determined how the idea would work and designed the behavioural probation form.

The grade 8 cohort was informed of this latest development and a letter was sent home to each parent notifying them of this strategy and how it worked. When a student committed an infraction or series of infractions, he/she is to be given a behaviour probation form. Everyday, for the next three weeks, he/she should have their teachers fill it out at the end of each class as stipulated on the form. At the end of the three-week period, the score is tabulated and if a student receives a score above the recommended grade, he or she will be taken off the probation. However, if a student scores less than the recommended grade, their parents are called in and together, attempts are made to work out a strategy to help the student. The guidance counsellor would get involved and other external bodies such as the Child Development Agency, depending on the situation. In cases of dispute, the school would seek help from the Dispute/Conflict Resolution Board.

The students did not like the idea of walking around with this form, nor did they want to be brought before the board. Additionally, there was an improvement in parental support as parents did not want to leave their jobs to attend disciplinary meetings; consequently, by the end of the school year, the grade 8 cohort became more settled.

FOOD FOR THOUGHT:

Discuss the importance of collaboration with external organizations to student development and the success of a school.

PART 3:

Classroom Management Tips

Recipes from My Classroom Menu

While there are several documented strategies for behaviour and classroom control, it must be pointed out that they are not applicable to all situations, classrooms and culture. Therefore, teachers must be vigilant and ensure that keen attention is given to their classes so they will know the needs and best practice strategies to apply to address these needs. Thus, it is fair to conclude that managing the classroom and student behaviour takes some amount of creativity, nurturing thought, and immersion into the student's world. Often as educators, we ignore the world in which our students live while the reality is, it is an understanding of this world that will give you the key(s) to reaching them. In managing the classroom, strategies are not cast in stone as the climate of each classroom differs and strategies applied are sometimes dependent on the lessons being taught. However, there are basic tips that can be employed to help you set a tone for your classroom for effective behaviour and classroom management. The tips in this section are taken from my personal classroom menu. They are flexible, and are quite applicable regardless of what is being taught. You must understand that I teach practical subjects, (dance & drama), hence, it is easy to lose class control. Sometimes the students get overly enthusiastic or they may sometimes display great apathy, but the former is more frequent.

Hope you will find them useful.

RECIPE #1:
Sharing Experience

This must be done at the beginning of your class. The students get a chance to say anything that is on their minds in three or four sentences. To ensure order, an object is passed around and only the student with the object is allowed to talk.

INGREDIENTS:
* Chairs/cushions/sitting space
* Small object e.g. ball

INSTRUCTIONS
33. Place chairs/cushions in a semi-circular fashion. When students enter, instruct them to sit (In my drama class students sit on the floor and I with them).

34. Introduce them to the activity. Give instructions and then introduce the ball.

35. Give the ball to the student who will start the activity (Sometimes as the teacher, it is comforting if you begin the activity. It helps to set the tone for the students). Remember the ball in hand, is a license to speak. Speaking without the ball in hand must attract consequences.

36. At the end of the sharing process when the ball gets back to you, give the students the final motivating tip (anything positive) and move on to your lesson.

    Please note, if your class is a large one, and you do not have much time to hear all, then you may:

    a. Let students select papers from a bag; or select various fruits from given ones, colours, etc… then you will let all the persons who selected specific fruits/colours to share in that session. Be flexible in the selection process.

    b. Ask students to volunteer. You may be surprised that someone has something burning on his or her mind and need an avenue to share it.

PURPOSE:

The purpose of this activity is to set the tone for your class. It gives you a chance to know where the students' minds are and the mood they are in. This will help you to better address them during your lesson.

Point to note: The first time I did this activity with a group of grade 8 students, one girl asked if she could step outside for one minute. I hesitated. She pressed further, "Miss, all I am asking you for is just one minute. Please." I relented. When she returned to class she just sat. As the class progressed, I gave her special attention without taking it away from the others. Whenever I explained things I would ask "Are you with us Marsha?" or "Do you under-stand Marsha?" I did it because during the sharing process, I realized she had something on her mind. At the end of the class she came and thanked me for allowing her to go outside for one minute. To date, I do not know what was wrong with her or what was on her mind but that one minute I gave her, may have very well saved us all some trouble.

RECIPE #2:
Musical Intro

This technique is a traditional one that has remained current and effective. From the days of slavery, the slaves used this to make work lighter, easier and more bearable. So, why not use it in the classroom for the same effect?

INGREDIENTS

- CD player/laptop (Instrument from which to play music)
- CDs or any other storage device with songs. (Ensure these are songs that your students will love, so be sure to do your research. It would be ideal if you can find songs that are relevant to the lesson you are teaching that day.)
- Speakers

INSTRUCTIONS:

29. Before your students get to your classroom, start playing the songs. That way they enter the classroom to the music. If you are lucky, you may find one bold student who will decide to dance. It is for this reason why as the teacher you must be on hand to monitor their entrance so this does not get out of control. Your presence will restrain them.

30. Engage them in a brief dialogue about any of the songs, focusing on the lyrics, story, the writer, etc. That way the discussion is meaningful and helps them develop critical thinking skills informally.

31. Do your housekeeping, e.g. marking the register with the song as background music.

32. Proceed with your lesson.

33. If your students stay with you in the same space all day (like in the primary school) this can still happen. Just let them line up by the door, start playing the music, then let them enter the room.

PURPOSE:

Students coming into your classroom all come with different energies and you need to ensure that you contain those energies and focus them all in one place. By playing the music and discussing it briefly, you have already arrested their attention and put everyone on the same page and in the same frame of mind. Additionally, it will give students the impression that you are abreast with the trends of their world and will make them more responsive to you.

Please note: While students are completing class work, you can also play music softly. This will calm them and reduce the talking. They will be too absorbed in doing the work and listening to the music.

The first time I tried this strategy, as they sat writing, I could see lips moving to the songs and heads bobbing slightly, but there was absolutely no talking.

RECIPE #3:
Sit in Their Midst

Most times it is customary for teachers to have a desk and chair at the front of the class that separates them from the students. As lessons are imparted, we often stand at the front and occasionally move around the room which is symbolic of authority or our superiority. However, there are moments when we should drop that symbolic action.

INGREDIENTS

- Open-mindedness
- Interactive skills
- Desire to share
- Intuitiveness

INSTRUCTIONS:

34. As you walk around the room, do not be afraid to take a seat in the midst of your students. Students like that. It makes them feel close to you. As you impart instruction, allow some of it to be articulated from within their midst. Sometimes to do this, you may have to displace a student (you can do this displacement at the beginning of the class or impromptu). Send that student to sit in your chair (ensure there are no personal items on your desk). The 'lucky' student tends to find it exciting to be selected to sit in the teacher's chair.

35. If you are conducting a class where students are doing individual or group presentations, this is the perfect opportunity to employ this strategy. You will be surprised to see the students preparing in advance, a seat for you in their midst. This will cause them to be more focused because they do not know where you will be sitting at any given time.

36. I have tried it, and students anticipate sitting in the teacher's chair. However, what I realized they liked more, was to have me sit with them. Do not do this every class you have. That way when it is done, it feels special. That is why it is good to have a menu from which to choose your strategies, so the students do not get tired of the strategies you are employing.

PURPOSE:

- Enable closer interaction with students
- Develop trust among the students
- Increase respect
- Facilitate closer monitoring of students' behaviour
- Make students more attentive
- Allow students to feel more appreciated

RECIPE #4:
Teacher's Pet

This is one of my favourite on this menu. A student who finds favour with a teacher or authority is often referred to as teacher's pet. But what is so wrong about finding favour with a teacher? It means you must be doing something right. Some persons do not share this view but I hope by the end of reading through this activity you will. This is the method where a student gets the privilege to shadow you for the entire class.

INGREDIENTS
* Criteria/rubric for teacher's pet

INSTRUCTIONS:

37. Students must be aware of the criteria from the beginning of your class or the moment you decide to implement this.

38. Once you have all your criteria, let the class add two or three more to it. That way they aid in the decision making process.

39. Together, outline what will be expected of the individual who is selected as teacher's pet (make sure tasks are exciting). You can also attach a merit system to this. If a child earns this title two or three times, a merit is awarded and so on. Be creative in the reward system you attach to this.

40. Ensure the criteria are written in their books, or placed in a clearly visible position.

41. At the beginning of a class, announce who the teacher's pet will be and ask students to remind you of the roles. Please note, you can also allow students to cast their votes at the end of the previous class, and it is those votes that determine who the teacher's pet will be. Some teachers may opt to let students wear a nicely made sash (if it is a boy, a cape perhaps) during

class or for the rest of the school day announcing this position. The important thing is, make a big deal out of it. If you don't, then the students will not buy into it. Sell it to them so they realize the importance of it and aspire to achieve it.

POSSIBLE CRITERIA

For a student to be considered for this position he or she must:

- Be disciplined, respectful and obey both school and classroom rules.

- Take on leadership roles without being prompted to do so and carry out these leadership responsibilities without fear or favour.

- Be responsible and dependable students to whom the teacher could entrust tasks and they were carried out with efficiency.

- Complete and submit assignments on time even if they were incorrect.

- Be always early for school and class.

- Maintain an average of no less than seventy percent (70%); (remember that this is just a suggestion), work very hard and has never been afraid to seek assistance.

Please note: I included the part about not being afraid to ask for assistance because sometimes students sit in our classes and they do not understand some things, but for one reason or another, they are afraid to ask for help.

You get the gist. You can add to this list based on the needs of your class.

PURPOSE:

- Encourage students to uphold the rules of the school and class
- Promote leadership abilities
- Improve communication skills
- Encourage hard work

RECIPE #5:
Movie Time

Did you know that students enjoy seeing themselves on the television? It is for this reason that I have a recipe on my classroom menu called movie time. This is where I would record different activities in class and play them back for students to see themselves.

INGREDIENTS

- Audio-visual/multimedia equipment
- Appropriate activities
- Check list of what will be reviewed on the tape
- Rules governing the review (playback) process

INSTRUCTIONS:

27. Set up your recording device.

28. Assign tasks to students. Inform them this task will be filmed/recorded and will be viewed following class.

29. Record activity. If the recording instrument is something that students are allowed to handle, you can also let them assist in the recording process if the nature of the activity/task allows it.

30. The following class, or whenever you decide to show the video, set up your viewing equipment (TV, laptop, projector, etc…) before students come to class (if your class is stationery, then do this after their break or lunch so it gives you a chance to set up before they return to class).

31. When students arrive at class, remind them of the rules and then give them an outline of what the class will be looking for as they watch the video (it will be more effective if you assign specific things to specific groups of students

and let them give a report on it at the end of the video. That way they are sure to pay attention).

32. Show the video.

33. Sit/stand at the back of the class so you may observe all students as they watch the video.

N.B. **This strategy is most effective whenever you are doing class presentations. When you do the viewing of the recording, you do not have to watch everything, especially if it is lengthy and you do not have the time. In that case, be strategic in the ones you decide to show the class and be sure to explain to the students why you have done so. This explanation will eliminate feelings of hurt.**

PURPOSE:

- Engage students
- Keep them focused
- Increase enthusiasm
- Motivate them
- Reduce disruption
- Encourage robust and fun discussions
- Encourage meaningful dialogue instead of talking out of turn

Teachers can be flexible in their rules for this activity. Whenever I do this, students ask permission to take snacks to class as they want to create a real movie setting. I grant them such privilege if one, they maintain or surpass the standard behaviour; two, we agree on the type of snacks they can carry; and three, they agree that if garbage is left in the class, every student will receive a demerit. If they comply with the rules, they will become class of the week or month and this will be posted on the notice board for all to see it. However, please do not do this every class but often enough to achieve your objectives and keep students interested.

RECIPE #6:
Grouping Methodologies

"I do not like group work" is the common retort you will hear from most students, especially those in high schools. However, despite this aversion, they must be exposed to it as it is an important aspect of every child's development. As teachers, we must prepare them to be global citizens. We must emphasize the fact that in this global world, it is all about team work regardless of how one feels about it. Hence, we must ensure that a part of this preparation includes students developing the ability to work well with others – even those they think are not their friends. Additionally, this aversion sometimes results in classroom and behaviour problems. Teachers therefore must find creative ways to encourage group activities while managing the classroom effectively, and while imparting the necessary life skills that group work teaches. Here are a series of grouping methodologies that can be used in your classroom to achieve same.

#6A: GAME GROUPING
I will use a game of 'Atoms'. It's very good for creating groups.

INGREDIENTS
- List of leadership criteria
- Pool of games appropriate for the objective

INSTRUCTIONS:
42. Give students instructions for the game.

43. Students will walk around the room.

44. While they are walking, teacher calls a number and students will then get into groups based on the number you called. Eg. the number four (4) students

will form themselves into groups of four. Normally, the student who is left out of the group will be out of the game. This rule however, will not apply since you are using it for a grouping strategy (unless you see how it fits into your grouping technique).

45. Repeat this about three times calling various numbers that will ensure all students fall into a group. The fourth time, call the number that you want each group to have. Once they have formed the groups, you end the activity and inform them that they will work in those groups.

46. Ask each group to select a group leader. To guide them in this process, you can give them some criteria that the group leader must possess, and the roles and responsibilities of the leader based on tasks you are about to assign.

PURPOSE:

- Erase bias
- Give students the opportunity to work with peers whom they may not have interacted with otherwise
- Develop their social skills
- Increase their capacity for teamwork
- Develop leadership capacity
- Develop decision making skills

#6B: PUSH-START GROUPING

Criteria: know the students in the class.

INSTRUCTIONS

34. Select four students to stand at the front of the class in a horizontal line (the starting number may change based on the number of students in your class).

35. Instruct each student to alternately select a second student who will stand behind them to start forming a vertical line (the students who started the selection process will be the leaders of each group).

36. Students will continue the alternate selection process, but they must consult with each other within their respective vertical lines to decide who will be selected to be a part of their group. This will continue until all students have been selected to join a group.

37. Assign tasks to students. Before they start working, prompt them to tell you the role and responsibilities of the group leader in the completion of this task. Observe the groups as they work. At the end of tasks, highlight the best leader and award leadership badge (this can be anything created by you). Remember, students enjoy being rewarded.

N.B. **If you have students who are not as popular with the class, either because they are too quiet, or too aggressive resulting in them being overlooked or the last person of choice, this grouping methodology is a good way to remedy the practice. This is because the teacher can choose those least likely to be selected first, as the individuals to lead the selection process.**

PURPOSE:

- Encourage decision making
- Develop negotiation skills
- Improve teamwork
- Improve communication skills
- Get everyone involved

#6C: LET THE FRUITS DECIDE

INGREDIENTS:

- Fruits (real or artificial)

INSTRUCTIONS:

38. Place the fruits in the open so students can see them (amount is based on the number of students you desire each group to have).

39. Students will select a fruit they like the most from what is on display (it is important to place a limit on the number of persons who can select a particular fruit. E.g. the first five).

40. After five persons (or your specified number) have selected a particular fruit, no other student can, so remove that fruit from the table.

41. After the selection process is over, put like fruits together. The group will then select a group leader.

42. Each group will be given the fruit selected. At all times during the activity/ task, the fruit must be visible and remain in good condition until the end of the activity/task.

Please note, for this this activity, you can use numbers, colours, or any object of your choice. Numbers will only be applicable based on your choice of object.

PURPOSE

- Improve decision making skills individually and as a group
- Improve capacity for teamwork
- Erase bias
- Promote collaborative strategy
- Make students more responsible
- Improve negotiation skills

ADDITIONAL TIPS:

Do not tell yourself that you are not creative. It is not a magic wand concept. It takes effort. It takes several times of getting it wrong and you reflecting and trying something new. There are several other things that you can try.

What is your **marking strategy**? Sometimes you can allow students to mark each other's work. This however is based on the nature of what you have given them to do. Is it group presentation/ short answers/ multiple choice? Trust them to do it.

Let them sometimes assist you with creating a rubric of assessment. When they do this, they are also better able to understand what is expected of them as well as mark each other's work. Do you have any idea the level of skills they would develop through these activities, while at the same time making the kingdom called classroom a pleasant place to be? Make them feel a part of the process but do not relinquish your role as teacher.

What is your **testing procedure**? Do you always take the paper pusher approach? What about a mini-oral test? Get creative with how you phrase the questions. E.g. create a section called **"Who am I?"** This is where you personify the subject. So you may ask a question such as: "**I am a sentence that compares two things without using as or like. Who am I?**" or "**I am the fictional role in a novel or play. Who am I?**" The student will then provide the answer. If it is a mathematics class you may ask: "**I have three equal sides, who am I?**" You can switch it around for whatever you want. It could be **"What am I?";** **"Where am I?"; "Where is this?"** among others. All you need to do is establish ground rules for this testing and make sure you reinforce them. That way students will take it seriously. This way you get a chance to test students' knowledge in an unconventional way; they learn in a fun way. Please note this strategy is applicable to all subject areas. You may sometimes want to give them the opportunity to work in small groups and set questions on particular topics to ask each other. This is perfect for revision. It also encourages students to utilize higher order thinking skills.

You can use music/sound effects with this activity. Have a pre-selected set of songs cued up. Use one student to do the selection if you want them to be more involved. When you ask the question and the students answer correctly, play a song or sound effect that is symbolic of being correct; when it is incorrect, play the song that is symbolic of it being incorrect. If the students are thinking, you can play the Jeopardy song. Very soon, they will catch on to the routine. When they get it right or wrong, they will start the song that is symbolic. This adds excitement to your class.

Planning will be an important part of executing some of these strategies. Classroom management and behaviour management will get easier with these techniques. Now go and create your classroom menu.

Happy teaching!

PART 4:

Workshop Simulation Activities Compartment

The education landscape continues to evolve. Thus it is the duty of educators to keep abreast with these changes and equip themselves with the necessary skills to effectively function in the world of the changes. Therefore, all school principals/ headmasters must ensure that continuous training and development is a part of the structure of their school's improvement plan.

However, in some instances, instead of seeing training sessions as an opportunity for learning, it is perceived as a chore; a mundane chore that triggers a sense of apathy within educators. Hence the trip to these sessions is sometimes like an unwilling bride or groom being dragged to the altar. This could be attributed to several things such as the design of the sessions, implementation, motivation and learning styles. Often, content is not a concern but moreso the presentation style of the various presenters asked to speak on specific areas. They tend to lose the attention of their audience and as a consequence, educators leave the seminar without gaining the requisite knowledge or skill that was intended for them. The truth is, like the students, teachers need to be actively engaged in the sessions. As a trainer, you have to let your 'hair' down, shed some inhibitions and set the tone of your presentation. It is like a performer. You go on stage, it is the performer's mandate to keep the audience enthralled, captivated and completely tuned in to their performance. Sometimes, the best mode for workshops and training and development sessions is an edu-tainment approach. This is where your audience is being educated and entertained at the same time. This can be easily achieved by using creativity and keeping teachers actively involved. What does this mean? It means that the persons charged with the task of organising and implementing, need to design the training sessions that can facilitate this. Part of the design include (identifying the need assessment, fulfilling the need, choice of speaker). I include need assessment because the staff must see the need that the training session is attempting to fulfil. If persons do not see the need/importance, you can expect resistance.

Below are a group of suggested activities that can be used in training and development sessions with educators.

Activity #1:
Follow the Leader

Explore leadership skills. The teacher is a leader and institutions must cater for this. As stated at the beginning of this text, the teacher is a manager – manager of time, people, processes, resources just to name a few. A good manager must be a good leader. Hence, this skill must continue to develop throughout a teacher's career. Educational institutions can help its staff develop this skill through professional development seminars. Here are some activities that are good for doing this.

PURPOSE:
- This teaches an individual to be observant; appropriate use of timing; be innovative; be in tune with the persons they are working with; follow directions; give directions; build relationships.

INSTRUCTIONS:
37. This can be done in pairs or as a small group of four or five; it would be good to use both so you can compare the response of the groups to the pairs.
38. Form small groups or get in pairs. A group of teachers must remain to be observers of the entire activity.

39. Face partner or members of group and stand about three feet apart from each other.

40. The facilitator will then select one person to be the leader and the others will be the reflection.

41. The leader will do a series of timely movements and the reflection(s) will attempt to mirror the movements with precision and timing to give the impression there is a real mirror.

42. After forty-five seconds or one minute, the facilitator will give instructions for the group to select a new leader. This time, they will select the leader of the group and repeat number four (facilitator and group of teachers observe how they conduct the process).

43. Repeat number five. End activity when you think you have seen enough. Do not draw it out too long. Participants will become bored.

DISCUSSION GUIDE:

- At the end of the activity, discuss it openly with teachers.

- Discuss how is it that individuals were able to follow the leader – focus on why were they able to follow or not able to follow.

- Did the leader do timely movements that were easily followed by the others? Focus on how the leader carried out directives given by the facilitator; what strategies did he/she employ to ensure the other group members were able to keep up, such as positioning of body, types of movement, pace of movement, etc.

- How effective did the group(s) make the transition from one leader to the next versus how the pairs did it?

N.B. This is just a guide for discussion. Facilitator must ensure he/she gets the perspective of the observers as well as the participants.

CONCLUSIONS DRAWN

All participants will now draw conclusions (either individually or in small groups) about:
- Characteristics of a good leader
- How leaders arrive at decisions

- Ability of leaders to follow and give instructions; strategies to help subordinates follow directions
- Differences in leading a small number (the pairs) versus a larger group (the group of four or five)

N.B. These are just some suggested conclusions. The discussion will spark others.

Activity #2:
Leader May I - Double Take

TAKE ONE

PURPOSE:
- This activity is good for teaching leadership styles, organization protocol, decision making, organization relationships, and communication skills.

INSTRUCTIONS:
40. Facilitator will ask for volunteers or find a creative way to get the number he or she wants, e.g. ask all the persons born in the months of June, July and August to stand (the number of persons selected will be dependent on the number of persons engaged in the training process).

41. Once you have your volunteered participants, assign each a number or you can use their names. Let them form an horizontal line if you have the space. If not enough space, find a creative way to have them stand based on your spatial capacity.

42. Facilitator would then call numbers or names randomly and give each a task; e.g. number one, please walk around the room and you have 30 seconds

to find someone who has been teaching for 12-15 years (facilitator must decide what tasks will be given to participants).

43. The participant who has been called will respond by saying "Leader may I"? The facilitator will respond "Yes you may" or "No you may not". If he/she says yes, the participant will carry out the task. If the response is no, the participant cannot proceed (leader doesn't have to provide an explanation for retracting instruction given). If the participant proceeds without saying "Leader may I", same individual will not be allowed to carry out the task.

44. Facilitator will end the activity when he/she sees fit and move on to take two.

TAKE TWO

Using the same group of participants or new ones, follow all instructions above but number four has a modification. If the leader says "No you may not" to a participant, same participant has the option of asking three questions to seek justification as to why given instructions were retracted. The questions may also be about the nature of the task given (discussion should not last longer than two minutes).

DISCUSSION GUIDE:

23. Conduct a general discussion about the activity.

24. Discuss leadership style in Take One – authoritative.

25. How appropriate is this leadership style for the organization? Is it in keeping with best practices in leadership and education management?

26. Feelings of individuals when rejected without explanation and its possible impact on organization development.

27. Compare leadership style in Take One to that of Take Two.

28. Is Take Two leadership style in keeping with the best practice in leadership and education management?

29. Did the inclusion of dialogue/discussion impact the protocol of the activity?

30. How did the discussion element impact the activity?

31. Look at the protocol to follow in carrying out activities and how this equates to protocol in the work place.

N.B. This is just a guide for discussion. Other details will come out of the activity. Facilitator must ensure he/she gets the perspective of the observers as well as the participants.

CONCLUSIONS DRAWN:

All participants will now be assigned tasks either individually or in small/large groups to draw conclusion about activity such as:

- Importance of leadership style to organization development
- Importance of dialogue for effectiveness
- Importance of organizational protocol

N.B. These are just some suggested conclusions.

Activity #3:
Let Us Do Craft

PURPOSE:

- This activity can highlight the importance of a deadline driven environment, power of teamwork, knowing individual strengths and weaknesses, knowing each other, discovering hidden skills/talents, self-regulation.

INSTRUCTIONS:

47. Facilitator will provide objects for this activity.
48. Participants will form small groups (if the group is very large, some persons could be making objects, others could be observers paying keen attention

to the process while ticking off a check list, one person could be a time keeper, etc.).

49. Each group will be given a set of objects to create something – maybe an egg holder or egg catcher, a scale, etc... participants can only use the objects provided by facilitator.

50. Facilitator will set the time limit by which participants should complete tasks.

51. At the end of the allotted time, facilitator will test each group's creation. E.g. if it is an egg holder, facilitator will drop an egg into it.

DISCUSSION GUIDE:

- Conduct general discussion about the activities.
- Discuss how well did persons work as a team.
- Did a leader or different leaders emerge during the task?
- Strategies employed by each group.
- Level of participation by group members.
- Importance of meeting deadlines.
- Did all the groups complete tasks within the given time frame?
- How did groups react to the time limit?

CONCLUSIONS DRAWN:

All participants will state conclusions drawn about:

- Importance of teamwork
- Impact of working in a deadline driven environment
- Consequences of working under pressure
- Possible reasons for not meeting deadlines and consequences

N.B. These are suggested conclusions. Participants may come up with others.

Activity #4:
Do As I Say

PURPOSE:
- This activity can be used to explore communication and interpretation skills. Additionally, it emphasizes listening skills and the importance of giving clear and precise instructions.

INSTRUCTIONS:
45. Facilitator will instruct participants to take out pen/pencil and paper (facilitator may also provide these).
46. Participants will listen carefully to what is said by facilitator and carry out that task on paper.
47. Participants cannot look at each other's paper.
48. Facilitator will then describe a picture that he/she has and the participants will draw the image based on their understanding of the instructions (facilitators will decide the type of picture).
49. At the end of instructions, facilitator will reveal his/her picture to the participants.
N.B. **The facilitator may opt to divide the participants into small groups, select a leader for the group and give him/her an image to present to the group. That way there will be one main facilitator and co-facilitators for the activity. At the end of the activity, groups can discuss instructions given by various facilitators.**

DISCUSSION GUIDE:
- Conduct a general discussion about the activity.
- Compare images drawn by participants with that of the facilitator.
- Assess similarities and differences and discuss what accounts for them.
- Ascertain whether persons were able to complete the image and discuss what accounted for successful completion or lack thereof.
- Discuss the clarity with which the instructions were given.

CONCLUSIONS DRAWN:

All participants (individually or in a group) will now draw conclusions about the activities based on the discussion. Conclusions can be drawn about:

- How persons interpret information
- Importance of communicating instructions clearly
- Listening skills

ACTIVITY #5:
Let Them Highlight It and Solve It

PURPOSE:

- The purpose of this is to let teachers be a part of both needs assessment identification and problem solving solutions. It also assists in the identification of strengths and varying competencies; improves critical thinking skills, encourages dialogue and collaborative practices; encourages public speaking skills, negotiating skills, broad-based planning and participation.

INSTRUCTIONS:

50. Facilitator will group participants or give them the opportunity to place themselves into small groups.

51. Each group has 10-15 minutes to identify two to three challenges that the institution/organization is facing and provide two solutions to solve them (facilitator can also give groups specific areas, e.g. behaviour management challenges, academic challenges, etc.).

52. At the end of the fifteen minutes, the designated speaker for each group will present the information generated by the group.

DISCUSSION GUIDE:

- Conduct a discussion about the information presented.
- Were there any recurring challenges identified by the various groups?
- Discuss the severity or urgency of the challenges.
- Explore the feasibility of the solutions posited.
- Explore the next steps to the challenges identified.

CONCLUSIONS DRAWN:

In groups or individually, draw conclusions about:

- Effectiveness of team work
- Importance of broad-based participation
- Effectiveness of group problem solving techniques

ACTIVITY #6:
Transition Leader

PURPOSE:

- The main purpose of this activity is to highlight the importance of succession planning. Additionally it focuses on communication skills, delegation of tasks, leadership skills, self-regulation/time management skills, social skills and personal competences.

INSTRUCTIONS:

32. Participants will form small groups based on facilitator's instructions.
33. Each group will select a leader (main rule is that, there must be a leader by the end of the completion of the task).

34. Facilitator will call all leaders together and instruct them with tasks for each group (each group will be given a specific time by which to complete the task).

35. The leaders will then return to their groups and communicate information about the task to the members.

36. Halfway during the task given, facilitator without notice, will withdraw the leaders from the groups. The rest of the group members will have to continue with the task without the leader. No additional time will be granted to complete task.

DISCUSSION GUIDE:

At the end of the activity, conduct a discussion with participants.

- Were the groups able to complete the task without the leaders? Explore why or why not.

- Did the groups experience any challenges after the leaders were withdrawn? Explore challenges experienced or reasons there were no challenges.

- Were there initiatives taken within the groups after the leaders were withdrawn?

- Examine how the leaders' withdrawal would affect each group if it was a small organization.

CONCLUSIONS DRAWN:

Individually or collectively, participants will now draw conclusions about:

- Importance of succession planning and state ways of doing it

- Importance of communicating clear and precise instructions

- Importance of keeping abreast with developments within an organization

Exploration Activity: Select any case from the previous sections and design a developmental workshop plan utilizing these simulation activities, or devise some of your own.

N.B. These are just suggestions for discussions and conclusions. Explore the others as you proceed.

Go plan, execute and enjoy.

You Made It!

If you are reading this page, then it means you opened this briefcase, and leafed through many pages to get here. Congratulations. You made it...to the end. It is the hope that you were inspired, and the 'light bulb' in your head is shining brilliantly because of the number of ideas floating around in your mind.

Remember, no educator is perfect. Being an effective and efficient educator/administrator is a process which involves possibly making tons of mistakes and using those mistakes as the ultimate teacher. It takes years of experience to develop a high level of expertise; however, with the right approach and scaffold, you can accelerate this process. Prospective and recently licensed educators, you are not about to walk into a bed of roses but you can make it a walk in the park. Experienced and veteran educators, you will not be able to fix all the woes in the education system but you can certainly initiate and inspire change.

"Each of us desires to share with others our vision of the world, only most of us have been taught that it is wrong to do things differently" (John Biggs) but this is not true.

As educators we need to remember that we are agents of change and we must share our visions for positively transforming lives. However, change is only possible when we open ourselves to existing and pending possibilities. A part of that openness is to release inhibitions that we have placed on our capabilities.

Allow creativity to run its course. Use it to paint colourful trajectories that touch and change lives.

Educators must think creatively and critically to constantly develop new strategies to best serve our students and each other, to efficiently cope in the fast paced, changing world. Because there is no one best way, educators must find what works best for them. Due to the fact that you are all teachers and not cheaters, you will work towards impacting change. What is clear however, is that you all have the capability to be not just a good teacher but a great teacher. This book has clearly outlined cases, tips and techniques that provides a scaffold for you to achieve this greatness.

So, go try your cases, testify, 'cook' a lesson, stimulate others...you are now officially an education manager!

REFERENCES

Chaffee, J. (2000) "Thinking Critically" Houghton Mifflin Company.

Evertson, C & Weinstein, C. (2006) "Handbook of Classroom Management: Research, Practice and Contemporary Issues" Lawrence Erlbaum Associates.

Gorton, R et al (2007) "School Leadership & Administration: Important Concepts, Case Studies, & Stimulations" McGraw Hill.

Marzano, R et al "The Critical Role of Classroom Management" Retrieved from http://www.ascd.org/publications/books/103027/chapters/The-Critical-Role-of-Classroom-Management.aspx May 16,2014.

APPENDICES

Sample Rubric Case Study Assessment:

Teacher/Peer/Self Evaluation

Here is a suggested rubric that educators could use as a form of assessment for the cases. This is not cast in stone as the facilitator may opt to add or remove some of the assessment points.

Participant's name: _________________________________   Date:______________

Evaluator: ____

	Always	Usually	Seldom	Never	Not Applicable
Identify and understand issues in the case					
Give appropriate solutions and recommendations to issues					
Match issues in case with rules in Education Code					
Match issue in case with rule in Child Care Protection Act					
Summarize case effectively					
Insightful and thorough analysis of issues in the case					
Excellent response(s) to colleagues comments					
Demonstrates exceptional knowledge of education issues					
Demonstrate excellent knowledge of effective administrative approaches					

Comments: ____

____

____

BEHAVIOUR PROBATION FORM INITIATIVE BY SU-AN DALEY OF GAYNSTEAD HIGH SCHOOL

DAY: FRIDAY   DATE: ....

TIME	T	R	I	A	Teacher's Signature	POINTS - For Official Use
8:00						
8:45						
9:30						
11:00						
11:45						
12:30						
1:15						
TOTAL						

The student will not be allowed to participate in any sports or extracurricular activity while on probation.

Student should receive an average of 252 - 280 points at the end of the probationary period which will reflect the 90% compliance rate targeted to avoid a meeting with the Disciplinary Committee.

The student will be given a maximum of THREE weeks to remove the probation by improving his/her behaviour and/or attitude.

GAYNSTEAD HIGH SCHOOL
BEHAVIOURAL PROBATION
SHEET

STUDENT'S NAME :...

GRADE :...

PROBATION PERIOD :....................................

The probation sheet is designed to reform students who have flagrantly or repeatedly violate any of the school's regulations.

Students MUST present probation sheet to teacher at the beginning of each class and collect it at the end of the class

DAY: MONDAY   DATE:...................

TIME	T	R	I	A	Teacher's Signature	POINTS - For Official Use
8:00						
8:45						
9:30						
11:00						
11:45						
12:30						
1:15						
TOTAL						

DAY: WEDNESDAY   DATE: ....

TIME	T	R	I	A	Teacher's Signature	POINTS - For Official Use
8:00						
8:45						
9:30						
11:00						
11:45						
12:30						
1:15						
TOTAL						

DAY: TUESDAY   DATE: ....

TIME	T	R	I	A	Teacher's Signature	POINTS - For Official Use
8:00						
8:45						
9:30						
11:00						
11:45						
12:30						
1:15						
TOTAL						

DAY: THURSDAY   DATE: ....

TIME	T	R	I	A	Teacher's Signature	POINTS - For Official Use
8:00						
8:45						
9:30						
11:00						
11:45						
12:30						
1:15						
TOTAL						

KEY
STUDENT'S CONDUCT

T = Completes assigned task
R = Respects authority
I = Positively interacts with peers
A = Appropriate behaviour/attitude displayed

CONDUCT	POINTS
E - EXCELLENT	10
G - GOOD	7
F - FAIR	5
P - POOR	1

Know Yourself and Where You Stand

*Cheater Versus Teacher

(*This phrase was coined by education administrator, writer, & editor Alcia Morgan Bromfield)

WHO ARE YOU?

CHEATER	TEACHER
Does not plan lessons	Plans engaging lessons
Consistently late for school & classes	Adheres to time
Has no expectation/targets for self, class and students	Sets targets and works towards achieving them
Thinks he/she is the best and not open to growth	Knows his/her strengths and weaknesses and works towards constant strengthening and development
Uses a dictator/authoritarian approach	Collaborates
Ignores students	Listens to students

Good Teacher Versus Great Teacher

Now that you have discovered who you are, you now need to determine the type of teacher you are. Several educators had this to say about 'good teachers' and 'great teachers'. What about you? Better yet, which are you?

A good teacher can impart the knowledge, practices and behaviours that a student needs to be successful in exams and graduate from school with honours. A great teacher instills in the students the love for knowledge, the quest for betterment and a high sense of self worth in the students. They do not try to be perfect or above the students, but show human and emotional connection with their students. A great teacher is a guide.

Gavin Myers

Good teachers adhere to the allotted time mandated by law. Great teachers go beyond the call of duty and go beyond the allotted time mandated by law.

Good teachers tell you to express yourself, chastise the outspoken and are wary of the thoughts of a smart brain. Great teachers encourage self-expression, admire the courage of the outspoken and love the thoughts of a smart brain.

Good teachers have high expectations of students. They teach and leave the rest for the students to finish. Great teachers extract from students more than they thought they had to give.

Good teachers recycle lesson plans. Great teachers find different ways to teach a topic each year.

Good teachers research and find new information and strategies for his/her class. Great teachers share best practices.

Dorraine Reid

Good teachers teach lessons. Great teachers teach life! As a student, the folks who stand out in my personal experience as great teachers all have one thing in common: their influence and impact went beyond the lessons. They inspire, not intimidate. They build up instead of tearing down. I've had some 'good' teachers who made me want to pass the exam just to prove them wrong. I've had some 'great' teachers who make me want to be the best even now...because they showed that belief in me.

Owen 'Blakka' Ellis

Great teachers inspire students to go and do. Great teachers are not afraid of challenges. They show passion and ignite passion among their students. Great teachers take satisfaction from seeing the 'light bulb' go off in their students' heads! Great teachers dream of ways to share knowledge!

Alcia Morgan Bromfield

A good teacher consistently exceeds the expectations of the institution and regulations; a GREAT teacher creates new and higher expectations of himself and his students, TRULY believes these can be accomplished and are worth accomplishing, willingly makes the plans and personal sacrifices necessary for him and his students to accomplish these expectations, and in the end would have been remembered as someone whose practice transformed his students, colleagues and the teaching craft for good!

Liston Aiken

The good teacher shares information well and ensure students learn. The great teacher inspires the students to seek info, share and discuss and apply the knowledge to everyday life.

Rayon Simpson

Great teachers focus on developing persons for tests beyond the classroom; good teachers help students to pass academic tests.

Alvin Allen

A great teacher is a person who will do anything for her students. She will go the extra mile to influence a child's life in a positive way. A great teacher lives for her students! A great teacher treats all her students fairly! A great teacher researches and finds ways to help all students. A great teacher listens and learns from students. A great teacher has sleepless nights to plan for students' success. A great teacher does not look for things in return. A great teacher uplifts students and never gives up on students. A great teacher just teaches and doesn't think about the money! A great teacher treats teaching as a Christian ministry instead of a job! A great teacher leans on God for guidance! A great teacher touches lives! A good teacher is just a good teacher, they hardly touch lives!

Casandra Salomon

Qualities of a Good Administrator

IS THIS YOU? ADD SOME MORE TO THIS LIST.

- Effectively puts the pieces together

- Aware of what is happening in the school

- Keeps an open door

- Makes firm and good decisions

- Respects ALL staff members

- Handles conflicts well

- Motivates staff

- Inspires staff

- Always collaborates

- Keeps up with best practices

- Knows strengths and weakness of staff and uses them for development of institution

Meet the Author

Dorraine Reid is an excellent educator and is considered one of the best in her field. She has taught at all levels of Jamaica's education system. She holds a Master of Science Degree in Public Sector Management from the University of the West Indies. Her Bachelor of Science Degree in Education Administration was conferred by Western Carolina University, and she earned a Diploma in Drama in Education from the Edna Manley College of the Visual & Performing Arts.

During her years as an educator, she has served in various capacities which include classroom manager, lecturer and resource person for drama/theatre arts for the Ministry of Education. She has also served in the capacity of secretary of the Jamaica Association of Dance and Drama Educators. Because of her outstanding work and unconventional but highly effective methodologies, she is highly sought after as keynote speaker for several primary and secondary schools' development seminars, and has organized and implemented several training workshops for her colleagues.

Dorraine is a trained and active theatre practitioner who is a member of the multiple International Theatre Institute Jamaica Chapter Actor Boy award winning theatre company the Independent Actors Movement. She is also known for her strong technical skills in light, sound and stage management.

As an excellent event planner, extra-ordinary coordinator, meticulous researcher, and a trained and active theatre practitioner, Dorraine is equipped with the skills to create and execute unforgettable and life changing projects. She has excellent knowledge of curriculum design and writing. This she garnered from her extensive work with the Ministry of Education's Core Curriculum Unit in the re-drafting of the National Standards Curriculum (NSC). She has also written courses for training agencies. Her articles on current affairs and education have also been published in Jamaica's two daily newspapers, the Gleaner and the Observer. Additionally, she has written various poems, written and arranged songs, as well as published academic papers on the Social Science Research Network. She currently hosts an active blog on issues related to education at *http://educatorrainereidinspires.wordpress.com/*. You can learn more and keep up to date with her work by following her writer's Facebook page "Reid & Write with Dorraine".

www.ingramcontent.com/pod-product-compliance
Lightning Source LLC
Chambersburg PA
CBHW051831150726
47998CB00001B/372